James Madison

James Madison
Creating the American Constitution

Neal Riemer
Drew University

Congressional Quarterly Inc.
1414 22nd Street N.W.
Washington, D.C. 20037

Printed in the United States of America

Library of Congress Cataloging in Publication Data

Riemer, Neal, 1922-
  James Madison: creating the American Constitution.

  Bibliography: p. 183
  Includes index.
  1. Madison, James, 1751-1836—Contributions in
political science. I. Title.
JC211   1986   321.8′092′4   86-16512
ISBN 0-87187-405-9

To
David and Ellie
Jeremiah
Seth and Barbara

Acknowledgments

I should like to acknowledge my intellectual indebtedness to some very stimulating teachers: Arthur N. Holcombe, Louis Hartz, Benjamin F. Wright, Carl J. Friedrich, and Charles McIlwain. They understood so well the democratic experiment of 1787.

Similarly, I want to acknowledge with deep appreciation three friends, keen students of both American and democratic thought, whose bright presence I sorely miss in this bicentennial year: Clinton L. Rossiter, David Spitz, and Robert G. McCloskey. I also want to thank Frank Sorauf and Mitchell Morse, long-time friends and former colleagues, for their constructive substantive and literary criticism of an earlier draft of this book.

Additionally, I want to acknowledge two outstanding Madisonian scholars: Irving Brant, whose splendid, multivolume biography of Madison has done so much to restore Madison to his rightful place in our history; and Douglass Adair, whose magnificent detective work has so brilliantly illuminated crucial influences on Madison's political theory.

Finally, I want to thank Joanne D. Daniels, director of CQ Press, and David Tarr, director of Congressional Quarterly's book department, for helping to bring *James Madison* back to celebrate the bicentennial of the Constitution; Maria Sayers and Nola Healy Lynch, who skillfully guided this revised edition through publication; and Evelyn S. Meyer, head of Drew University's library reference department, for her assistance in responding to my requests to check out bibliographical materials.

Preface

In this book I have tried to illuminate the political theory of James Madison. I have made the central question of this study the basic problem that Madison faced in his lifetime: Is republican government in a large state possible?

In Chapter 1, I have tried to introduce the reader to this problem and to the circumstances and approach that conditioned Madison's lifetime response. How could one achieve the more nearly perfect republican union in the light of four major difficulties that plagued the infant republic—disunion, large size, faction, and the anti-republican danger? Madison's approach stressed the values to which republicans were committed, the political realities which might limit or advance such values, and the feasible public policies which might prudently maximize republican objectives as political circumstances shifted.

In Chapter 2, I have sought to probe more fully the republican dilemma of reconciling liberty and large size: by identifying Madison's ideological commitments, by noting the absence of historical guidance in connection with this dilemma, and by exploring Madison's understanding of human nature.

In Chapter 3, I have focused on Madison as a *nationalist* who saw in a greatly strengthened, more nearly perfect union the instrument to cope with the danger of *disunion,* both in 1787 and in the 1820s and 1830s. In Chapter 4, I have emphasized Madison as the *Federalist* defending the new principle of federalism as the republican answer to the problem of *large size.* In Chapter 5, I have stressed Madison's role as an *empirical political scientist* who articulated an explanation of how *faction,* the disease of liberty-loving republics, might be brought under control in an extensive federal republic. In Chapter 6, I have highlighted Madison the *democrat,* who was passionately concerned with the *anti-republican danger,* and who worked his way toward what I call a theory of democratic politics, a theory based on the significance of civil liberties, bold republican leadership, and a republican political opposition. Finally, in Chapter 7, I have attempted to match Madison's political theory against a model of modern democratic theory in order to assess the continuing viability of Madison's realistic and pluralistic approach to politics.

My central concern has been with Madison as political theorist, rather than with Madison as Secretary of State or as President. My hope is that the varying aspects of the man that I have emphasized—philosopher-statesman, republican scholar, prophetic nationalist, prudent federalist, empirical political scientist, constitutional democrat—will add up to a picture of our most creative political theorist.

Contents

Chronology

1787-88   Co-authors *The Federalist* papers with Hamilton and Jay.

1788   Argues powerfully for the new Constitution in the Virginia Ratifying Convention.

1789   Elected to U.S. House of Representatives, after being defeated for U.S. Senate. Serves until 1797. At first assumes leadership in House on behalf of Washington's Administration. Introduces Revenue Bill and Bill of Rights.

1791   Tours North with Jefferson. Publishes first essay in Freneau's *National Gazette*. Attacks Hamilton's proposed Bank of the United States.

1792   Breaks with Hamilton. Becomes major Republican leader opposing Federalist party. Writes essay in *National Gazette* attacking Federalists.

1793   Writes "Helvidius" papers, in reply to Hamilton's "Pacificus," criticizing Washington's Neutrality Proclamation.

1794   Marries Dolley Payne Todd.

1797   Retires to private life at Montpelier.

1798   Authors Virginia Resolutions, attacking Alien and Sedition Acts.

1799   Reenters Virginia House of Delegates and defends Virginia Resolutions in his "Address to the General Assembly" and in his 1799-1800 Report on the Resolutions.

1801   Chosen by President Jefferson to serve as Secretary of State. Remains secretary for Jefferson's two terms. Exercises great influence in shaping basic foreign policies of the United States: in acquiring Louisiana, in resisting France and England via diplomacy and economic pressure (embargo), in defending the freedom of the seas, in preparing for the acquisition of Florida.

1808   Elected President of the United States.

1809   Inaugurated as President.

1809-12   Recommends increase of American armament. Issues proclamation announcing the United States' possession of West Florida. Seeks honorable settlement with Great Britain, but builds popular support for war if British remain unrelenting.

1812	Asks for Declaration of War against Great Britain. Reelected President.
1813	Inaugurated as President for second term.
1813-15	Fights to maintain national unity and to build economic, military, and naval strength to win Second War for Independence.
1815	Sends treaty of peace to Congress. War ends.
1817	Vetoes Bonus Bill to aid internal improvements. Retires from Presidency to Montpelier.
1826	Becomes Rector of the University of Virginia upon Jefferson's death.
1828	Nominated as a presidential elector.
1829	Serves as delegate to Virginia Constitutional Convention.
1830-36	Warns of the perils of nullification. Urges all to cherish the Union.
1836	Dies June 28.

Introduction

As we reflect, almost two hundred years after the event, on the creative breakthrough in political theory and practice that resulted in the Constitution of the United States, it is particularly appropriate to examine the political theory of James Madison, a major architect of that document. Madison, I argue in this book, should be seen not only as the political philosopher of the Constitution of 1787, but properly as the prophetic political philosopher of our republican constitution as it evolved during the first five decades of the life of the American nation.

Madison was not only a major architect and resourceful champion of the strengthened instrument of 1787, which he so decisively helped to shape in Philadelphia and so persuasively defended in *The Federalist* papers and in the crucial Virginia Ratifying Convention; he was also the author in 1789 of the Bill of Rights, and a leader in the first Congress in Washington's first administration. And we must not neglect his role in the 1790s in opposing some measures of the Federalist party, particularly the Alien and Sedition Acts, and his warnings at the end of his life against the perils of nullification. In the light of these contributions—and keeping in mind, too, his services as Secretary of State and as President—we can appreciate Madison's broader role as philosopher-statesman of a strong and effective republican constitution that embraces the concept of equal rights for all and special privileges for none; that fashions a government of broad but limited powers; that allows a vigilant but loyal opposition to function; that is dedicated to federal union as the necessary basis of the republican experiment.

As we reflect today on the vicissitudes of democratic destiny—and on the crises of war, genocide, tyranny, poverty, environmental degradation, and nuclear catastrophe that we have known in the twentieth century—it is heartening to turn to Madison and the generation of 1787 for prophetic inspiration about the values, understanding, and judgments that might wisely guide us in the future.

However, even as we celebrate the bicentennial of the Constitution, let us not exaggerate. Madison and his generation were by no means perfect. In some respects—for example, in their attitudes and behavior toward Native Americans, Blacks, and women—they illustrated a narrowness common in their day. Nevertheless, on a crucial range of issues—involving the principles, organization, and conduct of free and popular government in a large country—they demonstrated the continued vitality of the tradition of prophetic politics. They demonstrated a commitment (1) to such prophetic values as freedom, justice, and constitutional order; (2) to criticism of threats to such values; (3) to constitutional action to bridge, or at least narrow, the gap between republican aspirations and existential realities; and (4) to continuous scrutiny and futuristic projection to safeguard the more nearly perfect Union that they created in 1787. Madison was one of the keenest of this prophetic generation.

Madison's political philosophy was soundly based on a tough-minded concept of human nature, modified by a qualified confidence in people and buttressed by certain natural safeguards and auxiliary precautions possible in an extensive and representative republic. Madison realized that the makeup of human beings is an amalgam of depravity and fallibility *and* virtue and wisdom, that a political philosophy predicated solely on sinners or solely on saints is foredoomed to failure.

In his political philosophy Madison realistically acknowledged the clash, accommodation, and cooperation of a wide variety of interests as the very heart of a free society—a society we today call democratic. But, recognizing the struggle of interests, Madison proposed not to abolish struggle but to employ the multiplicity and diversity of interests in an extensive and representative republic on behalf of necessary freedom and of legitimate authority. Madison's theory would protect both justice and limited government without sacrificing republican rights and popular rule.

Madison correctly held that the struggle for power and the likelihood of abuse of power should make citizens highly suspicious of both the entrenched and enriched classes and the enduring and impoverished masses. Monarchy, aristocracy, oligarchy, plutocracy, mobocracy, theocracy—all these are undesirable and unsafe. But if the will of the majority in an extensive and representative republic is the safest will, the majority nonetheless can abuse power. The rights of individuals and groups must be preserved, regardless of who threatens such rights: majority or minority. It is always proper to take alarm at the first threat to the nation's liberties; and, if necessary, to engage in bold and sometimes "radical" action to secure such rights.

Yet, recognizing the limitations of people, the dangers of faction, and the shortsightedness of instant majorities, Madison argued that there still must be strong and popular government. Zealous devotion to the basic rights of individuals and groups—due process of law and freedom of religion, of speech, of press, and of communication—must be matched by devotion to strong, efficient, able, soundly established government capable of coping with common problems. And as Madison knew that revolution is an ultimate weapon that may be employed as a natural, or moral, right to safeguard republican liberty and rule against intolerable oppression, so radical political reform may be necessary to obtain a new constitution adequate to the demands of a more nearly perfect union.

As we today reassess the continuing vitality and validity of Madison's political philosophy, we need to be aware of both its strengths and its weaknesses, some of which we have already touched upon. Madison's ability to take advantage of diversity, conflict, and size in the United States of 1787 is a major strength of his political philosophy. He undertook a keen empirical analysis of faction and of the clash of interests in the struggle for power and policy, and he demonstrated that a well-constructed republican government can regulate those interests on behalf of the common good. His generally pragmatic view of national power is another strength. Power, he argued, will ebb and flow in response to common need and the ability of government to satisfy such need. Madison's devastating attack on those who would muzzle a loyal opposition is a third strength. A fourth strength is Madison's brilliant critique of the misguided friends or foolish foes of strong, republican, federal Union. Madison's devastating critique of the Articles of Confederation is the dramatic early case in point. Less known, but equally prophetic, is Madison's critique of Calhoun's doctrine of the concurrent majority. Calhoun's doctrine, Madison argued, must lead either to anarchy or tyranny or civil war. Madison's perceptive analysis of Calhoun's doctrine has still not received the recognition it deserves.

On the other hand, there are weaknesses in Madison's theory. Its central weakness, some may argue, is perhaps its underlying negativism. His theory may explain satisfactorily why no one faction can unite and dominate the government; but, by the same logic, it can also explain why "good government" by the right people may also be obstructed. Madison did not adquately demonstrate the way in which a "neutral sovereign" (his term) would be able to govern in the public interest. Some critics do not find entirely satisfactory his reliance on a system of representation to produce legislators devoted to the common good. Other critics hold that Alexander Hamilton's political theory (despite Hamilton's plutocratic bias), by emphasizing as it does vigorous presidential leadership, left a better legacy that could be employed by a powerful but democratic government on behalf of the public interest. Still other critics question Madison's overly narrow interpretation of national power in the 1790s and challenge his perhaps dubious reliance on ultraconstitutional interposition in defense of freedom against an alleged national tyranny.

Other weaknesses are also apparent: for example, Madison's lack of greater precision in identifying the faction whose unjust actions are to be controlled; his failure fully to appreciate overlapping, and sometimes conflicting, factional membership; his dubious assumption that somehow the public interest would emerge from the clash of contending and powerful interests in a republican, representative, and extensive republic; his questionable belief that representation and indirect elections would indeed refine the popular will.

Yet when all is said and done, we may grant that the theory of the extensive, federal, representative republic has worked reasonably well. The feasibility of republicanism in a large state has been demonstrated. The party system (which Madison and Jefferson helped to establish in the 1790s) has emerged as a bulwark of constitutional liberty; the contest of free parties has strengthened freedom instead of contributing to factional strife and to the other pessimistic prophecies of classical political thought—mobocracy, anarchy, tyranny, and civil war. With the possible (and important) exception of the Civil War, these prophecies have not been fulfilled.

Madison's political philosophy constitutes a remarkably creative and prophetic quest for a more nearly perfect Union, a Union both strong and free, dedicated to natural rights and based on republican principles, and possessing significant power to protect the common weal. Madison's political philosophy is, in many respects, still wonderfully fresh in its appeal and modern in its application. It has proved to be a highly workable "proximate solution" to the never-ending "insoluble problem" of wise and effective human governance.

To a fuller examination of Madison's political theory we can now turn.

James Madison

CHAPTER 1

Political Theory and
Prudent Guidance

> " . . . If any constitution is to be established by delibera-
> tion and choice it must be examined with many allowances,
> and must be compared not with the theory, which each individ-
> ual may frame in his own mind, but with the system which it is
> meant to take the place of; and with any other which there
> might be a possibility of obtaining."
> — 5 *Writings* 49 (1787) (To Archibald Stuart)

I

Is republican government in a large state possible? This
was the momentous question which faced modern democracy
at its birth in America. This was the central question that
challenged the political genius of James Madison, America's
first great political scientist. What political theory would
provide guidance for republican statesmen struggling with the
problem of reconciling liberty and authority in the New
World? How could one maintain free, strong, and popular
government in the huge expanse of the American domain?

In 1776 the eloquent words of the Declaration of Independence announced to all mankind the rationale of the first
great democratic revolution of the modern world. But the
Declaration advanced little beyond John Locke, England's
outstanding seventeenth century political philosopher, in
articulating a theory of limited, responsible, representative
government for the new eighteenth century American experiment in a large republican state. In 1781, two years before
American victory in the Revolutionary War for Independence, the infant republic adopted the Articles of Confederation. This frame of government was expressly designed to tie

together more securely the thirteen states which sprawled some fifteen hundred miles along the Atlantic Ocean from what is now Maine to Georgia, and some six hundred to twelve hundred miles from the Atlantic coast to the Mississippi River. But could this large American empire—whose component states exercised substantial sovereignty—be successfully organized according to the republican principles of the Articles of Confederation?

Madison did not think so. He recognized that the older constitutional tradition of Locke was not fully relevant to America's unique republican environment and geographical circumstances. He perceived, too, that the government of the Articles of Confederation had not been effective in overcoming America's difficulties. As Madison surveyed the scene in the late 1780s, four related difficulties hindered the achievement of sound republican government. These were disunion, faction, anti-republicanism, and large size. The potent forces of disunion were strongly entrenched in the thirteen jealously "sovereign" states. Selfish factional interests—groups opposed to the nation's common interest—operated within each of the states and sought to obstruct the central government of the Union. Men and movements unsympathetic to republicanism were also potentially dangerous. They were hostile to popular government in theory and disgusted with the weakness and degradation of republican government in practice. And finally, the large geographic size of the United States increased the threat to free and effective republican government. It did so, ironically, by encouraging both those who favored almost complete autonomy for each state and those who advocated great centralization of power in the Union's government. Thus those who endorsed decentralization were inclined to play down strength for the Union in order to ensure liberty in each state. And those who approved of consolidation were disposed to regard liberty for men and states less highly than authority for the nation.

Madison refused to be impaled on either horn of this age-old dilemma. He sought, instead, in 1787 to work out a new theory which would successfully reconcile broadened conceptions of liberty with expanded notions of authority. To achieve the more nearly perfect republican union—with strength at the center and freedom at the circumference—Madison advocated a *new* kind of federal government. He supported a new constitution which would bolster the necessary powers of the central government and limit the discordant activities of the thirteen states. He enunciated the saving virtues of an extensive, federal representative republic. He thus developed a political theory which would serve as a prudent guide to action for those seeking to ensure the success of the republican experiment in harmonizing liberty and large size. This theory would include ethical commitments in the republican tradition and, in certain areas, notable religious freedom, a generous expansion of republican liberties. It would involve an empirical explanation of how the new federal republic would indeed function to advance the republican ends of freedom and union, happiness and power. And it would make clear the principles and patterns of wise leadership that might be prudently followed.

A just and full estimate of Madison's contribution to republican theory in a federal state of large size cannot, however, concentrate solely on his most creative period, that time involving the writing and the adopting of the Constitution in 1787 and 1788. The difficulties of disunion, faction, anti-republicanism, and large size persisted. They were not eliminated with the establishment of Washington's first Administration in 1789, or with Jefferson's presidential victory in 1800, or with the Republican Ascendency that extended through the first three decades of the nineteenth century. These difficulties, often in new historical contexts, reappeared and forced Madison to apply and develop his theory. Consequently, my treatment of Madison's political theory—which guided his career as a republican statesman until his death in 1836—will be based on the evolving thought of his entire life. This evolution will thus underscore those maturing political conceptions—including a bold assertion of civil liberties, the organization of a republican political party, and a strategy of constitutional interpretation—that would safeguard union and freedom against anti-republican attack.

I will, therefore, concentrate on Madison's political theory as an evolving response to the republican dilemma in the New World. However, I will also endeavor to see wherein

3

Madison's theory contains ethical principles, empirical explanations, and prudential insights which transcend the immediate history of his tempestuous times and which relate, descriptively and prescriptively, to modern America.

II

Despite his great contribution to the resolution of the republican dilemma in the New World—and despite the continuing validity of his political theory for modern political science—Madison remains the least popular and the least understood of the towering founders of the American nation. Initially, it is not easy to understand why this is the case, for—superficially—there seems to be concern for Madison's problems and recognition of Madison's role in grappling with these problems. Thus from 1776 and 1787 until today Americans have sought to reconcile liberty and authority, balance center and circumference, and curb both the selfish friends and the scheming foes of republicanism. This quest for a more perfect republican union has been a central quest of American political thought. And, clearly, Madison's solid contributions to this quest have not been unappreciated.

Thus, not many begrudge him the title "Father of the Constitution"; nor do they forget his coauthorship of *The Federalist,* deny his sponsorship of the Bill of Rights in 1789, overlook his fight against the Alien and Sedition Acts (1798-1800), ignore his service as Secretary of State (1801-1809), or close their eyes to his two terms as President of the United States (1809-1817).

Yet, interestingly, those who call him "Father of the Constitution" are not always clear whether he is so called because of his magnificent feat in recording the debates in the Constitutional Convention of 1787, or because of his key role in shaping cardinal features of the new American constitution. And many political scientists, who have a nodding acquaintance with Madison's political ideas as expressed in the Constitutional Convention of 1787, are often surprised to discover after fuller exploration that he by no means had his way in the Convention, even on those issues that were closest to his heart.

Similarly, every schoolboy knows that, together with Alexander Hamilton and John Jay, Madison wrote *The Federalist* papers and that these papers are of major historical significance. Almost everyone recognizes *The Federalist* as superb propaganda in the campaign to secure ratification of the new constitution; as well-reasoned, masterful essays in political science; and as the most illuminating, most authoritative, most exploited, and most influential commentary on the Constitution that we possess. Yet Madison, the articulate and penetrating republican political theorist, is often lost sight of in the preoccupation with Madison, the tough-minded, realistic, conservative author of such brilliant essays as 10 *Federalist*. Often, superficial observers distort Madison's concern with economic class struggle as a primary basis of politics, and overemphasize his alarm at factional threats to sound and orderly government.

Other questions persist and contribute to distortions of Madison's theory and practice. Yes, Madison did introduce the Bill of Rights, but did he not do so reluctantly and after arguing earlier that such a bill of rights was really unnecessary? Yes, he did fight against the Alien and Sedition Acts, but are not the Virginia Resolutions tainted, somehow, with the odious doctrine of nullification and secession? And did not Madison in these resolutions adopt a severely limited interpretation of national power, a crabbed interpretation that could only lead to disaster for a nation requiring strength adequate to its growing needs? How, many wonder, could Madison, the powerful and prophetic nationalist of 1787, become by the late 1790s the narrow, pedantic advocate of states' rights?

As for Madison in high office: Was he not, as Secretary of State, a mere errand boy for Jefferson? Was he not, as President, a weak and ineffective armchair theorist who permitted his country to be pushed into a war for which the country was ill prepared, a war which gained none of the great objectives for which it was allegedly fought—the end of impressment, freedom of the seas?

To some, these difficulties of interpretation suggest a split political personality. On the one hand, we have *Madison the Federalist*. Here Madison is the protagonist of a strong and vigorous central government. He is the enemy of the

5

power of the thirteen states. He is a foe of the abuse of majority rule. He is an ally of Hamilton. He is an early leader of the Federalist party. On the other hand, we have *Madison the Republican.* Here Madison is the antagonist of the expansion of Federal powers—and of special-interest legislation on behalf of the wealthy. He is the author of the Bill of Rights. He is the champion of the rights of states. He is the friend of rightful and reasonable majority rule. He is a partisan of liberty against authority. He is a general in the army of Jeffersonian Democracy. So the duality of personality might occur to the superficial observer who has wrenched certain facts thoughtlessly from the complex context of a man's career in a dynamic society.

Indeed, this characterization might be extended by comparing Madison's views before and after his becoming President. The point here would be that the Federalists lost the electoral battle but won the policy war. And the generalization that would emerge from Madison's career would be this: The "outs" always criticize the "ins" for policies which seem more plausible when the "outs" themselves gain power!

These partial views suggest the need for a more balanced and more just perspective. In this study I shall strive for such a perspective. I will attempt to do so by seeking to clarify the fundamental purpose, cardinal principles, underlying logic, and enduring significance of Madison's political theory. Such an examination of Madison's struggle with the problem of popular, free government in a large country may, I hope, dispel much of the misunderstanding that still surrounds his thought. And it may thus make possible a more just appraisal of his political theory as perhaps the most fertile contribution to American—and perhaps also to modern democratic—political science that has yet appeared.

But what other reasons account for the fact that Madison is still the least popular and the least fully understood founder of the American nation? We long have had a Washington monument and a Jefferson and a Lincoln memorial in our nation's capital, but only belatedly (1980) a building (an annex to the Library of Congress) commemorating Madison. We have a Jefferson-Jackson day dinner, but Madison's name has not yet been linked with those democrats. John C. Calhoun is still often called America's greatest political theorist, although his claim—as I shall suggest—was long ago demolished by Madison's own penetrating criticism.

Folk heroes emerge best when they can be clearly identified. Washington: Revolutionary War general and first President of the new nation; Jefferson: author of the Declaration of Independence and towering Republican leader; Jackson: military hero and the common man's President; Lincoln: Great Emancipator and the savior of the Union. These identifications, of course, belie the complexity of the man and his times. Nonetheless, they provide myths to feed our ideological hunger. Madison, a judicious political scientist, refused to be identified with a simple or extreme position, whether it concerned nationalism or states' rights. And this led to explanations that hardly enhanced his popularity.

Thus, Madison's break with Hamilton in 1790, on the question of Federalist policy, spoiled his *Nationalist* image for the Federalists who lost little time in explaining away Madison's defection. Ironically, this Federalist effort also prevented Madison's emergence as the great *Republican* leader. It was difficult for the Federalists to present Madison as a man who was deliberately seeking to ruin the national credit or subvert the Constitution. His reputation for wisdom, stability, and integrity prevented this. So did his record as one who had labored long and hard to establish a stronger union. Consequently, another course was taken. He was pictured as a weak and timid soul who had been seduced by the devilish Jefferson. To compound the misconception, the Jeffersonians did little to correct this distortion because it served to make Jefferson look even better as a brilliant leader of republican forces. Thus what started as a "big lie" in the heat of partisan politics became a "lasting misconception" when the historians and biographers took over from the politicians.[1]

Other developments late in Madison's life—in the 1820s and the 1830s—prevented him from becoming the idol of the advocates of states' rights and slavery, and thus a folk hero of the *Southern* cause. Madison refused to defend slavery as a positive good. He condemned nullification and secession. He would not permit his attack on the Alien and Sedition Acts to be used by the pro-slavery hotheads of the South to disrupt

7

the Union. In determining the basis of suffrage in the Virginia Constitutional Convention of 1829 he favored a compromise between persons and property, which had the practical effect of favoring Westerners in the House of Delegates and Eastern slaveholders in the Senate—a compromise which failed to please either the slaveholders or their opponents. Madison's consistent refusal to endorse the pro-slavery states' rights position of John C. Calhoun or Robert Y. Hayne was explained away on the basis of Madison's falling away from the virile position of his earlier Virginia Resolutions. He had grown weak and old; he was no longer the strong and vigorous Madison of the Virginia Resolutions of 1798, 1799, and 1800. Thus, since Madison's strong stand at the turn of the century could not be denied, his later "apostasy" was charged to physical debility.

Consequently, as a result of these developments, Madison was denied the folk image of a great *Nationalist,* or a great *Republican,* or a great states' rights *Southerner.*

But there are still other reasons which may account for the relative neglect and misunderstanding of Madison's political theory and influence. First, Madison, alone, produced no great political treatise. Second, he possessed a great but not a brilliant gift of language. Third, he did not have a charismatic personality. And, fourth, he lived in a generation of remarkably gifted men, in whose company even a giant of splendid talents might often be eclipsed.

First: Madison left us no systematic exposition of his political philosophy. Unlike Plato, Hobbes, Locke, or Rousseau, and like his good friend Jefferson, Madison wrote more as an active politician in response to the exigencies of politics—and never consciously for philosophy, for arts and letters, for science and morals. More than any of the acknowledged masters of political thought, Madison talked or wrote about practical political projects. His response might involve the defeat of a bill in Virginia requiring religious assessments (1785), or the adoption of the Constitution (1787-1788), or the battle against the Alien and Sedition Acts (1798-1800), or the fight against nullification (in the late 1820s and 1830s). Like most of the Constitutional Fathers, his thought must usually be extricated with great scholarly caution from the political labyrinth. And most often his political theory must be appraised in the light of a dynamic political process which makes a basic consistency difficult and a foolish consistency absurd.

Moreover, Madison had little time for systematic political exposition in his earlier political career when he was shaping ideas to guide the embryonic nation in grappling with pressing political tasks. And, in later years, as an old man, he had little disposition to reformulate the political theory which had guided him and the republic so successfully for more than three tempestuous decades. In his youth Madison was too busy attending school in Virginia, or at the College of New Jersey (now Princeton). As a young man he was caught up in the turmoil of the Revolution, the struggles of Virginia politics, and the anxieties of a nation-in-the-making. Later he had little opportunity to set forth his maturing political ideas in a comprehensive work. There was too much to be done as a young state legislator; as a bright Congressman from Virginia in the government of the Confederation; as a planner of, and recorder and debator in, the Constitutional Convention; as an early leader—while in the House of Representatives—of Washington's first Administration; as the subsequent chief of the Republican opposition to the Hamiltonian Federalist programs in Congress; as Jefferson's Secretary of State for eight years; and as President for eight more, including several during (what some have called) the Second War for Independence. These public duties dwarf but should not conceal his role as farmer, amateur scientist, and husband. After he left the White House, his philosophic position had solidified; consequently, he was less concerned with theoretical innovation or systematic elaboration than with the defense and consistency of his ideas. In addition, his widespread correspondence with most of the key figures of his day, his generous hospitality, his duties in running his estate, and his agricultural, educational, and humanitarian work kept him occupied. He worked closely with Jefferson in founding the University of Virginia and succeeded Jefferson as Rector upon Jefferson's death on July 4, 1826. He was elected to serve in the Virginia State Constitutional Convention in 1829. And he was constantly being called upon for advice in connection with the issues of his day. These were among the duties of a man who was already sixty-five when he retired to private life at his beloved Montpelier.

Lack of single authorship—or of a unique and dramatic masterpiece—also makes it difficult to arrive more easily at a just estimate of Madison's thought. What many consider to be his major contribution to political thought was, of course, *The Federalist,* written with Hamilton and Jay. And although the authorship of these essays is pretty clearly agreed upon by key scholars, current editions still list several essays as jointly written by Madison and Hamilton; and Madison's distinct political theory in *The Federalist* is not always closely disentangled from Hamilton's. Madison also worked with Jefferson on many ideas and projects. Like his collaboration with Hamilton in *The Federalist,* Madison's partnership with Jefferson (whether in connection with religious liberty in Virginia, the emergence of the Republican party in the early 1790s, or the battle against the Alien and Sedition Acts from 1798 to 1800) has tended to blur Madison's original and sometimes differing views.

Second: If Madison was substantively no Aristotle, neither was he a literary giant. He was logical, tenacious, and clear in argument. His prose style is earnest and forthright. But he did not possess the rhetorical gifts of a Jefferson or a Paine. His writings convince but they do not take fire. His eloquence, as a speaker, was not like Patrick Henry's; he was no spellbinder. Only if eloquence is defined as the ability to persuade by convincing, would Madison be considered, as he indeed was by John Marshall, as "the most eloquent man I ever heard." [2] Madison's simple, unadorned, quiet style was convincing only to those who sought the illumination that his well-trained, clear mind provided. He would never mesmerize a mass audience or bewitch a nation.

Third: Americans also tend to ignore the political thinker whose personality is not striking, whose personal life and letters give little dramatic indication of his real historical stature, and whose more judicious manner prevents him from fighting his way forcefully into the romantic pages of history. Madison's judiciousness can be seen even in his bold effort to fashion a new constitution in 1787 and 1788. He has come

POLITICAL THEORY AND PRUDENT GUIDANCE

down to us in history as a prudent man of thought and not as a masterful man of action. His personality in the drama of history thus adds little verve or weight to his political message. No one would have dreamed of remarking of little "Jemmy" what someone once said of Daniel Webster: "No man can be as great as Mr. Webster looks!" [3]

The myth of Madison's innocuous personality is traceable in part to historical bias. But it is, I have also suggested, the result of his temperament, his simple literary style, and his not having a Boswell, a devoted biographer, who might have captured the flavor of his wit and charm in informal conversation. Oddly, the warm, bouyant, friendly Dolley Madison has unwittingly helped to perpetuate this myth by providing for romantic biographers a strong contrast to her presidential spouse. Madison's sobriety and probity also contrast sharply with the picture of his irresponsible stepson, John Payne Todd, whose drinking and gambling habits kept him constantly in trouble, and his parents constantly in anguish.

Fourth: Madison lived in the company of giants. Washington, Hamilton, Jefferson were masterful men whose character, statesmanship, and leadership moved the infant nation along the road toward successful independence, national strength, and healthy republican growth. In the shadow of these towering figures, one can more readily understand why Madison's own contributions to all these achievements are sometimes unfortunately overlooked.

The upshot of all this, I repeat, has been a popular and critical failure to appreciate Madison's major contribution to republican theory in what is now called a federal state and to the pluralist political science that is still so relevant to modern America. In recasting him as America's most creative republican theorist and first great political scientist, it is necessary to sketch in greater detail Madison's approach to political theory as a prudent guide to action.

III

For Madison, theory was intimately linked to practice. The function of theory was to provide the statesman with a prudent guide to action. Prudent guidance, however, must not

11

be confused with action itself or with a concrete, detailed program of action. A prudent guide to action is, of course, related to action and programs of action; but these are not identical, even though the philosopher-statesman is often required to cross the bridge from prudent guidance to programs of action and, then, to action itself. In understanding Madison as a theorist, the emphasis must be on the word *guide* or, perhaps, on philosophy, outlook, perspective. In Madison's case, such guidance involved a republican ideology to be advanced, the empirical propositions that explained why an "extensive republic" was indeed possible, and the operational principles that informed prudent practice.

The philosophical underpinnings of Madison's guide to action were, however, substantially unexamined. He developed no sophisticated epistemology—no learned understanding of the nature of the truth. He articulated no critical ethical theory—no penetrating account of individual and social values. He enunciated no comprehensive philosophy of history—no full-fledged explanation of movement and change in human affairs. Hence his guide would hardly stand up under the relentless analysis of the professional philosopher interested in epistemology, ethics, or laws of historical development.

Nonetheless, he did not lack perspective. He operated within the framework of a natural law outlook that was unquestioned for the most part by men of his age. This largely unprobed orientation—based upon a higher law, inalienable rights, social contract, and constitutional government—provided him with notions of truth and right and development in the domain of politics. Consequently, it is within the structure of this natural law philosophy that one must examine Madison's very definite ideas about the nature of man, of interests, of power, and of justice. These are the ideas which give more substantive content to his prudent guide to action.

Interestingly, optimism and pessimism were blended in Madison's historical outlook. He was influenced by Enlightenment hopes for rational progress toward freedom and happiness. He was also impressed—as a well-read student of history—by the short-lived nature of republican triumphs. Guidance, then, is to be understood as republican guidance provided in the light of an enlightened natural law philosophy and a limited, if meaningful, reading of republican experience in classical and western thought.

But what is meant by "prudent" in the phrase "prudent guide to action"? In brief, prudence is practical wisdom. It is that quality of mind which is concerned with wisely relating means to ends. It is the judgment essential to sound decisions in the everyday affairs of men. Madison did not develop an elaborate view of prudence, but it seems clear from his occasional comments and from his actions that he had grasped its meaning and its importance in politics.

Thus he understood well that theory, abstractly and dogmatically conceived, is unreal and can be mischievous. He insisted that certain "pure" theories were erroneous or dangerous. This judgment was, he perceived, true of "pure democracy." "Theoretic politicians" who have patronized "pure democracy" have erred in thinking that "by reducing mankind to a perfect equality in their political rights, they would, at the same time, be perfectly equalized and assimilated in their possessions, their opinion, and their passions." But, alas, Madison concluded, experience disproved this supposition.[4]

Madison's adverse criticism of "pure" theory was not a chance remark directed solely at "pure democracy." It was a fundamental criticism of "pure" theories along the line. Devotion to ideas of "pure" separation of powers, or "pure" undivided sovereignty, or "pure" laissez-faire, or "pure" universal suffrage, or "pure" perpetual peace—these, too, were concepts that had to be brought into a workable relation with experience, with feasibility, with probability.

Thus on laissez-faire: "The champions for the 'let-alone policy' forget that theories are the offspring of the closet; exceptions and qualifications the lessons of experience." [5]

Thus on perpetual peace: "A universal and perpetual peace, it is to be feared, is in the catalogue of events, which will never exist but in the imagination of visionary philosophers, or in the breasts of benevolent enthusiasts." [6]

Thus on universal suffrage: "It would be happy if a State of Society could be found, in which an equal voice in making the laws might be allowed to every individual bound to obey them. But this is a Theory, which like most Theories, confessedly requires limitations and modifications, and the only question to be decided in this or in other cases, turns on the particular degree of departure, in practice, required by the essence and object of the Theory, itself." [7]

Madison's prudential disposition engages the sympathy of realist and statesman, but it cools the ardor of mythmaker and dogmatist. Exceptions and qualifications, limitations and modifications—these are the ingredients of the democratic politics of civility, not the authoritarian politics of fanaticism. Madison's prudential politics also placed a high regard on probability, possibility, and timing.

Almost always Madison insisted on the need to "keep within the compass of human probability." [8] Dogmatic theory might propose but practical experience would most often dispose. Prudence required that circumstances, timing, and consequences be considered. In judging an issue, one must decide not on the basis of abstract theory but on the basis of political realities and feasible alternatives.

And so, in connection with the compromises dictated by the need to achieve agreement on the proposed new constitution of 1787, Madison declared: " . . . If any constitution is to be established by deliberation and choice it must be examined with many allowances, and must be compared not with the theory, which each individual may frame in his own mind, but with the system which it is meant to take the place of; and with any other which there might be a possibility of obtaining." [9]

The question of timing is perhaps best known in connection with the successful move to achieve the new constitution of 1787. The question was this: In "what mode and at what moment" ought the experiment in remedying the defects of the Articles of Confederation be made? [10] However, the question of timing was in fact an early and a continuing concern throughout Madison's life. His first great lesson in timing was learned in connection with his and Jefferson's efforts to advance the cause of religious freedom in Virginia. In 1779 Jefferson had eloquently, but unsuccessfully, attempted to secure passage of a Bill for Religious Freedom. But it was not until 1785 that Madison was able to kill Patrick Henry's proposal for religious assessments and, then, to maneuver, with the tremendous boost from his own "Remonstrance and Protest Against Religious Assessments," to enact Jefferson's bill. Here timing and political skill resulted in a signal victory for human liberty and marked a major step toward the First Amendment. Still later, Madison was patiently to employ proper timing in foreign affairs (an area in which he has not traditionally been considered at his best) to advance America's vital interests.

Always, Madison insisted, the consequences must be considered. These might be the adverse consequences for religious liberty in giving the Virginia legislature the power to tax all for the support of religion. They might be the fearful consequences of anarchy under the government of the Articles of Confederation. They might be the intolerable consequences of tyranny under the Alien and Sedition Acts. They might be the dreadful consequences of disunion and civil war that would follow the triumph of nullification and secession. The consequences, Madison insisted over and over again in his lifetime, must be detected in the principle and the principle denied.

For Madison, the more nearly perfect republican union was the constant goal. The means used to attain this goal would, then, be wisely adapted to time, place, and circumstance. However, Madison's prudential approach to politics did not preclude bold leadership when the situation, as in 1787, called for bold leadership. Furthermore, bold experimentation founded on sound theory was perfectly legitimate.

Thus Madison asked rhetorically in the Virginia Ratifying Convention in 1788: Does not the state of the Union "call for the friends of republican government to establish a republican organization?" "A change is absolutely necessary. I can see no danger in submitting to practice an experiment which seems to be founded on the best theoretic principles." [11]

Similarly, the concept of prudence did not rule out strong opposition when the situation, as in the 1790s, demanded adamant political resistance rather than concession or appeasement. Here, in Madison's judgment, the threat to republicanism demanded a shift in means. A broadly nationalistic interpretation of congressional power must take a back seat in favor of a rather severely limited interpretation of national power. Hostility to the narrow preoccupations of the states

15

was not now appropriate. Instead, the sovereign people of the states must be encouraged to defeat unwise and—in the case of the Alien and Sedition Acts—unconstitutional legislation.

These considerations illuminate the problem of consistency in politics. The prudent approach to politics makes a superficial consistency difficult to maintain. Madison suffered here more than most men in public affairs because he possessed such a strong character and was very sensitive to the charge that he was a political chameleon.[12] How difficult it is to try to maintain a superficial consistency in means when one is, paradoxically, committed to a consistent prudential approach to politics! Obviously, the same kind of consistency that might be expected of the strictly armchair political theorist cannot be expected of the political theorist who has been lucky (or unlucky?) enough to test his theory amid the trial of political battle. Shifts in policy, then, seem almost inevitable—given a commitment to prudent guidance in politics, and changing political, economic, and social conditions.

Madison approved a national bank in 1787, turned against Hamilton's banking plan in the 1790s, but then after 1800 again accepted the national bank. His subsequent acceptance was based on the country's prescriptive acceptance. Such prescriptive acceptance Madison defined as the "uniform sanction of successive legislative bodies, through a period of years and under the varied ascendency of parties."[13] Madison considered the "question as to canals" and other federally supported internal improvements "decided," "because [they were] sanctioned by the nation under the permanent influence of benefit to the major part of it. . . ."[14] Earlier in his career Madison had sought a constitutional amendment to authorize such internal improvements. Now he declared that a "change of opinion" based upon experience and "the results of improved reflection" should not be censured but approved.[15] Prudential change, then, is not to be confused with unprincipled opportunism. So prudential postponement is not to be confused with weakness. A decision to avoid either war or submission need not be interpreted as timidity or indecision, as for example, in the period from 1802 to 1812. It might be practically wise, as Irving Brant has written, on the basis of the country's need for time for growth, to adopt a policy of "economic pressure and negotiation while the fast-growing nation gathered basic strength." [16]

Of course, prudence can become a slippery notion that might be used to whitewash certain thoughts and actions that cannot be readily or convincingly explained. Today many may still have grave doubts about a number of Madison's arguments and actions. They may have reservations about his restricted interpretation in the 1790s of key constitutional clauses. They may have qualms about his overly legalistic approach to foreign policy in the same period. They may have misgivings about the ambiguity and danger of his doctrine of "ultraconstitutional interposition," which he enunciated to attack the Alien and Sedition Acts.

However, if the commitment to prudence does not and cannot save one from the errors of judgment that man is heir to, it may suggest a helpful line of conduct in public affairs. It may suggest an approach more salutary than rashness on the one hand or timidity and indecision on the other.

But, in this appraisal of Madison's prudential approach to politics, we must not lose sight of the main point. The key point to stress is that prudence requires a wise and conscious adaptation of means to ends. The ends must always be kept in mind as the central goal of policy. Means, then, will vary with circumstances. But the means employed must be rationally chosen. And they must be rationally chosen with the best understanding we have of their consequences in relation to desired goals.

Obviously, political theory so viewed cannot be scientific, primarily because the partly unscientific element of practical judgment plays so prominent a part in it. Yet theory so viewed can be extremely fruitful if it helps the theorist consciously to relate guiding principles to political life. Such principles do not automatically solve problems, for political problems are not like puzzles that have determined solutions. However, such principles may make the exercise of political judgment easier and more rational.

Furthermore, theory so viewed is fruitful if it forces the theorist to relate means to ends, to understand the dynamic nature of political reality, and to perceive that theory may not only be altered by reality but may also alter reality. Differ-

17

ently put, then, Madison recognized political theory as a critical study concerned with providing guidance for men in working out feasible programs of action, programs designed in the light both of the limitations and the possibilities of empirical reality to advance consciously conceived values.

In appraising Madison's prudential approach to politics it is important to call attention to his recognition that political theory is largely shaped by three factors: historical experience (in theory and in practice), present circumstances, and the creative mind. In connection with the first factor it is clear that Madison was one of those men "who were peculiarly fitted by training and circumstances to adapt to their purpose such principles as time and use had sanctioned." [17] He "never ceased to believe that 'academic' learning furnished necessary guidance for the practicing politician." It is thus important to relate Madison's thought to the great western tradition of political philosophy in order "to define his service as chief theorist of the American Constitution." [18] As Douglass Adair has shown, Madison did draw upon past political theory and history. It is thus not accidental that Aristotle's maxim bulks so large in Madison's own approach to political theory: "Wherefore the legislator and the statesman ought to know what democratical measures save and what destroy a democracy. . . ." [19] Nor is it accidental that the phrase "extensive republic" (which figures prominently in Madison's political theory) occurs twice in Montesquieu's influential *The Spirit of Laws.* And it is not by chance that one of David Hume's key notions achieves a now classic formulation in Number 10 *Federalist.* Hume maintained that the diversity, multiplicity, and competition of interests in a large, federally organized state would help to guard against the evils of faction.

If, however, Madison did incorporate past political theory into his own theory, the selection was in large part guided by the unique historical circumstances of America. There had been nothing like the American experiment in past history. Consequently, past political theory and practice were in many respects irrelevant to the American scene. If Madison was sometimes zealously committed to key ideas, he never insisted, dogmatically, that a theory for democratic Greece or

18

republican Rome or constitutional England could automatically apply to popular government in America. Aristotle, Machiavelli, Calvin, Harrington, Locke, Montesquieu, or Hume might suggest "lessons," but they did not have solutions. Who in America was to adjust theory to American conditions? The unique American characteristics did not by themselves produce a new theory. Rather they challenged the political thinker to come up with a theory that would take into account a large expanse of land, the spirit of liberty and equality, the prevalence of local self-government, the widespread distribution of property, an enterprising economic spirit, a deeply rooted constitutional ethos, and some kind of federal division of powers. These circumstances, then, would vitally affect the theory and practice of the American political community.

But, Madison perceived, the American environment did not automatically produce the more perfect republican union. Here, then, one comes to the recognition that political theory is in part the product of an incisive, creative, synthesizing mind. Madison saw the need for a new kind of federal government and creatively utilized ideas which would not only establish a new federal union adequate to hold the American empire together, but would also safeguard republican rule in that union and in its component "sovereign" states. He foresaw the danger to both liberty and authority in the operation of factional interests in the states and in the central government. At varying periods in his political career, proponents of such interests threatened the rights of both persons and property, refused to give the union necessary political and economic powers, sought special-interest legislation for the wealthy, attacked freedom of speech and press, and promised to disrupt the union through nullification and secession. Creatively, he was able to respond to this danger by strengthening the national government, by organizing a political opposition that would safeguard republican principles and civil liberties, and by exposing the political insanity of nullification and secession.

The bold creativity of Madison's approach to politics is perhaps best expressed in the closing paragraph of Number 14 *Federalist*. Here, of course, he sought to defend a novel

19

experiment, not a prescriptive constitution. This passage suggests clearly that Madison, despite his selective use of past theories, his respect for history, and his hostility to dogmatic, or "pure," theories, was not afraid to try something new when the occasion demanded it. Past theory and history must be respected, but not slavishly worshipped. The status quo must be critically appraised and rejected if fundamentally defective. A new theory, consonant with a unique American reality, might call for a new republican model. This was the prudent suggestion of the creative republican theorist. So Madison pleaded for the new constitutional experiment. This experiment was based upon a theory which explained why the new federal, republican constitution would work. The new constitution was not, of course, the work of one man. Yet the significant fact remains that only Madison had formulated— out of past principles, present circumstances, and future hopes—a new theory which could provide reliable guidance for the new republic.

> Hearken not to the voice which petulantly tells you that the form of government recommended for your adoption is a novelty in the political world; that it has never yet had a place in the theories of the wildest projectors; that it rashly attempts what it is impossible to accomplish.... But why is the experiment of an extended republic to be rejected merely because it may comprise what is new? Is it not the glory of the people of America, that whilst they have paid a decent regard to the opinions of former times and other nations, they have not suffered a blind veneration for antiquity, for customs, or for names, to overrule the suggestion of their own good sense, the knowledge of their own situation, and the lessons of their own experience? To this manly spirit, posterity will be indebted for the possession, and the world for the example, of the numerous innovations displayed on the American theatre, in favor of private rights and public happiness. Had no important step been taken by the leaders of the Revolution for which a precedent could not be discovered, no government established of which an exact model did not present itself, the people of the United States might, at this moment, have numbered among the melancholy victims of misguided councils, must at best have been laboring under

the weight of some of those forms which have crushed the liberties of the rest of mankind.[20]

These considerations should prepare the reader for a better understanding of Madison's approach to the republican dilemma in the New World.

CHAPTER 2

The Republican Dilemma
in the New World

> *"The instability, injustice, and confusion introduced into the public councils, have, in truth, been the mortal diseases under which popular governments have everywhere perished. . . ."*
>
> — *The Federalist*, Number 10

> *" . . . Some celebrated authors . . . have . . . transfer[red] to a republic observations applicable to a democracy only; and among others, the observation that it can never be established but among a small number of people, living within a small compass of territory."*
>
> — *The Federalist*, Number 14

I

A fuller comprehension of the republican dilemma in the New World requires, first, that we identify at greater length Madison's ideological commitments; second, that we note the absence of satisfactory guidance in classical theory and previous political history; and third, that we set forth his views on human nature and behavior in politics.

By identifying Madison's ideological commitments it is possible, initially, to better understand the problems that would harass a thoroughly republican thinker as he sought theoretical means to advance the republican ends so boldly proclaimed to the world in 1776. These ideological commitments were by no means entirely new, original, and unique. Republican thought already had a long and an honorable history before Madison was born. One need only mention the names of Cicero, Machiavelli, Harrington, Milton, and Sydney to indicate the intellectual lineage which Madison, as a child of the classical and English traditions, was to inherit. Furthermore, the ideas which came to be intimately associated with republican theory had already achieved expression in such different thinkers as Aristotle, Polybius, Montesquieu, and Locke. Among these ideas were such concepts as rule by the many, constitutional government, and the mixed state. Involved also was a dedication to the liberty, competence, and virtue of the individual citizen. Another concept was the fear of the concentration and abuse of power. Still another was the commitment to justice and the common good. In brief, republican theory called for limited, representative, responsible government. Madison thus lived and wrote in a dominant ideological climate of opinion which had been substantially created before his own labors on behalf of republicanism started. His task, then, was not to originate or even to broadcast basic republican theory, but to perfect it in unique America.

Madison, who was born in Virginia in 1751 and who attended Princeton between 1769 and 1772, grew to young manhood in a colonial world which mirrored the Whiggish, and ultimately revolutionary, temperament of the colonies. His postgraduate reading and study at home, his minor revolutionary activities in Orange County, and his service in the famous Virginia Convention of 1776 correctly suggest his acceptance of the political theory of the American Revolution. This theory defended a people's right to revolt against tyranny and to establish anew a government based upon popular consent and dedicated to the protection of man's natural rights. A rightful government would be constitutional, limited, representative, and responsible. It would be based upon known, fair, and orderly rules worked out to achieve effective and regularized restraint upon the necessary power that had to be wielded in order to protect life, liberty, property, conscience, happiness, and the common good. It would make clear those actions which a government must not take and those areas which it must not invade, upon penalty of violating the contract which embodied the people's trust. The people would have a share, albeit indirect, in the process by which law, which affected all, was made. The government would be accountable to the sovereign source of power, the majority of people, through periodic elections. It would also be accountable before the ultimate bar of a higher law which held that governmental power was a public trust to be employed only in the fulfillment of justice and the common good. These republican and revolutionary ideas Madison shared with many others. Consequently, his own basic republican orientation seems to echo the familiar but still heartening commonplaces found in the Declaration of Independence, the Virginia Bill of Rights, the English Bill of Rights, and in the writings of John Locke and James Harrington.

Thus, for Madison, a republic was a government which derived "all its powers directly or indirectly from the great body of the people" and which rested "on the capacity of mankind for self-government." [1] "The people were in fact, the foundation of all power, and by resorting to them, all difficulties were got over. They could alter constitutions as they pleased." In republican theory, if not always in republican practice, it was "politic as well as just that the interests and rights of every class should be duly represented and understood in the public councils." It was also a fundamental republican principle "that men can not be justly bound by laws in making which they have no part." [2] A republican government was one which was "administered by persons holding their offices during pleasure, for a limited period, or during good behavior." Even during this "short duration of their appointments" to government, "the trust should be placed not in a few, but [in] a number of hands." [3] The "fundamental" and "vital " principle of such republican government was *"lex majoris partis,* the will of the majority"; and the "majority who rule in such governments" were regarded as "the safest Guardians both of public Good and private rights." Such majority rule, however, was not to be one of unlimited power. It was instituted to secure "life and liberty, with the right of acquiring and using property, and generally of pursuing and obtaining happiness and safety." Whenever the government should be "found adverse or inadequate to the purposes of its institution," the people have "an indubitable, unalienable, and indefeasible right to reform or change" it. [4]

"I profess myself," Madison declared in 1788 in the Virginia Ratifying Convention, "to have had a uniform zeal for a republican government. If . . . [anyone] conceives that my attachment to this system [the new Constitution] arises from a different source, he is greatly mistaken. From the first moment that my mind was capable of contemplating political subjects, I never . . . ceased wishing success to a well regulated republican government. The establishment of such in America was my most ardent desire." [5]

Madison was thus deeply committed to a republican political ideology. Despite the weaknesses of the central government under the Articles of Confederation, and even though Madison was gravely disturbed by the possibility of unjust majority rule, primarily in the states, he worked faithfully and diligently for a new, yet republican, constitution. Madison consistently held that certain republican principles and devices were necessary in order to guard against monarchy, aristocracy, oligarchy, and plutocracy—as well as against mobocracy. Thus, he advocated popular ratification of the new constitution in order to secure not only a more legitimately republican union, but also a more effectively republican union. He favored the principle of limited tenure of office. He also endorsed the guarantee of a republican form of government to the states in order to "defend the system against aristocratic or monarchical innovations" and to make sure that the states "shall not exchange republican for anti-republican constitutions." He defended an electoral system which would permit the electors to be the great body of the people. "Not the rich, more than the poor; not the learned, more than the ignorant; not the haughty heirs of distinguished names, more than the humble sons of obscurity and unpropitious fortune." Speaking of the requirements of candidates for the House of Representatives, he declared that no "qualification of wealth, of birth, or religious faith, or of civil profession is permitted to fetter the judgment or disappoint the inclination of the people." Fairly consistently, he supported what he himself called the republican principle of majority rule and firmly opposed minority rule based on force, money, or birth. A bill of rights which Madison introduced in the first Congress provided yet additional protection against anti-republican onslaughts. Laws unlimited in their duration he opposed as "dangerous to republican principles." Even titles for the President and Vice President he opposed as "degrading appendages." This opposition was meant to "show to the friends of Republicanism that our new Government was not meant to substitute either Monarchy or Aristocracy, and that the genius of the people is as yet adverse to both." The only true *"cement* for a Union of republican people," Madison held, was a "republican policy throughout." [6]

In summarizing Madison's republican ideology, materials have been drawn from several periods in his life, extending from his entry into politics until the 1830s. It seems clear on the basis of the entire record that the general republican ideology that Madison brought to the Constitutional Convention in 1787 had been pounded into shape in the heat of the American Revolution out of older classical, continental, and British materials, and was to maintain substantially the same shape throughout his entire life. If, then, Madison's dominant republican ideology was not original, why spend time on it at all? There are three main replies to this question. First, understanding this republican ideology helps to dispel doubts about Madison's bona fide commitment to republicanism. Second, understanding this ideology helps us to better understand why Madison would devote his creative intellectual and political energies to the challenging task of adapting the traditional republican house to fit the unique American scene. Third, such understanding helps us appreciate Madison's unique contributions to republican theory—contributions which advance beyond the traditional republican ideology of his day: his conception of genuine religious liberty, his articulation of a new republican system in federalism, and his theory of a republican political opposition.

II

Writing in 1830, Madison declared: "The rights of man as the foundation of just Government had been long understood; but the superstructures projected had been sadly defective." [7] In this sentence he was calling attention to the fact that the founders of the Republic did not make their primary contribution to republican theory in terms of the rights of man, but rather in terms of the theory and practice of self-government in a large state. If brief, basic republican ideology was generally accepted. What was needed was a sound superstructure to ensure those rights. The republican dilemma, simply put, was that of adapting republicanism to a large state.

It is true, of course, that American experience from 1776 to 1787 had demonstrated the actuality of republican government. But that experience was not entirely a happy one. Indeed, it is almost miraculous that the union of the thirteen rebelling colonies was maintained from 1776 until the adoption of the Articles of Confederation in 1781. Despite all that revisionist historians have written to redress our traditional image of the weak and bumbling government under the Articles of Confederation, the important fact remains that the government was not, in the judgment of many keen and prophetic republicans, the more nearly perfect union which they correctly recognized as essential to safeguard republicanism in the New World.[8] Could such a republican government prevail without the pressures which had held the union together in the fight for independence? Would earlier loyalist cries of republican license prove to be tragically true? Was it not, indeed, necessary to strengthen the republican union by giving it the powers essential to the commonwealth?

But how was this to be done? What republican models would guide such a republican reconstruction? Here, when republican thinkers, such as Madison, looked for republican precedents, they found little or nothing. Past revolutionary and republican theory, as well as their own colonial experience, had aided them when it came to the defense of the revolution, the establishment of independence, and the temporary ordering of their own state and national affairs. But now, farsighted republicans were disturbed by the unhappy thought that the Articles of Confederation were not adequate to the task of establishing a more nearly perfect republican union. On the problem of establishing republican government in a large state, previous republican thinkers were either silent or pessimistic. Presumably, republicanism and empire were incompatible. Indeed, the long-term maintenance of republican government seemed a delusion.

Here the great classical models were silent. Aristotle, for example, had little or nothing to say about a republican federal state. Aristotle did, of course, endorse constitutional government as the best practicable government. Such a polity, or moderate democracy, embraced the notion that rule was to be in the public interest and for the common good rather than in the special interest and on behalf of a single individual or factional group. Government was to be one of law and not of men. Constitutional government was to be based on the consent of willing subjects and not on coercion or fear. In all this, Aristotle was a good reinforcement for British Whig doctrine. Madison undoubtedly gleaned from this same classical tradition a healthy respect for the middle class (then largely composed of farmers) as the backbone of a polity. The yeoman farmer could be relied upon. He was too intelligent to be victimized by demagogues. He was independent in mind and pocketbook. He was not envious of the rich and he would not be envied by the poor. He was mature in judgment, competent in public affairs, and virtuous in character. Constitutional government was safe in his hands. Madison may also have absorbed from this same source a number of other lessons. He may have learned to love justice, to hate faction, to admire a balance of social and economic classes, to respect political change, to appreciate sound public opinion, to understand the connection between economics and politics, and to believe in the possibility of using one's will and intellect to maintain a desirable state of political affairs. Yet he could have found little or nothing about a federal polity comparable to the actual political situation he faced in America.[9]

Madison may have read in Cicero a definition of the Commonwealth as "the people's affair ... the coming together of a considerable number of men who are united by a common agreement about law and rights and by the desire to participate in mutual advantages." He may also have found in Cicero a conception of natural law which had become so deeply embedded in western thought that it had become a basic premise of constitutional theorists in the sixteenth, seventeenth, and eighteenth centuries. Cicero spoke eloquently of a true law which men might know by reason, an eternal law which "summons men to the performance of their duties," an unchangeable law which "restrains them from doing wrong," a law which cannot morally be invalidated by human legislation, a higher law to which the state and its rulers are subject. But, again, there was in Cicero and in most other advocates of natural law nothing on a large federal commonwealth.[10]

And what of Niccolò Machiavelli whom James Harrington had called "the only politician [i.e., "statesman"] of later ages"? Had he read Machiavelli's *Prince,* Madison would have been impressed by Machiavelli's distress over Italy's "dissensions." And had he read the *Discourses,* he would have reacted favorably to Machiavelli's argument in favor of a united, strong, virtuous republic. Machiavelli had insisted that such a republic rests upon a virtuous people, government under law, a balance of social and economic classes, the healthy exercise of public opinion, and liberty resulting from a conflict of parties. To all these ideas Madison would have been receptive. But, again, in Machiavelli's republican model, that of republican Rome, Madison would have found little or nothing to help him in erecting a plan for a federal republic.[11]

James Harrington's contention that a commonwealth was the inevitable form of government for a country in which the whole people were landlords, or at least in which there was a widespread distribution of land, would have stiffened Madison's republican backbone. Harrington's conditions for a commonwealth fitted America perfectly. His insistence, with Aristotle and Livy, that a commonwealth must be an "empire of laws and not men" and must be dedicated to the interest of mankind would undoubtedly have reinforced Madison's republican convictions. Yet Harrington threw little light on the possibility of a federal commonwealth. The same was true of Harrington's countryman, John Locke. Locke had also expressed ideas of limited, responsible, representative government which were primary components of the dominant ideology of the American Revolution upon which the Constitutional Fathers built. Locke, of course, was only one among many who had expressed such ideas. But neither he nor such influential republican thinkers as Algernon Sydney had treated the crucial problem of a federal republic.[12]

Of the political thinkers better known to us today, only Jean Jacques Rousseau and Johannes Althusius, who were apparently not influential in America, and Charles Louis de Secondat Montesquieu and David Hume, who were, had touched directly and indirectly upon the problem of federalism. Both Montesquieu and Hume, it seems reasonably clear, had "lifted the veil from the venerable errors which enslaved opinion, and pointed the way to those luminous truths of which" they "had but a glimpse" themselves.[13]

The "way" in Montesquieu was neither direct nor comprehensive. Indeed, at first glance there seemed to be no "way" at all. Montesquieu had maintained that it "is natural for a republic to have only a small territory; otherwise it cannot subsist." This argument grated harshly on republican ears in America. If Montesquieu was correct, one could either assume (contrary to fact) that America was indeed a small state and hence safe for republicanism, or abandon hopes for republicanism in America. But was Montesquieu correct? And, even more to the point, was he of a single mind on this subject? Apparently not, for elsewhere in his famous book he had called attention to the virtues of the "confederate republic." He had emphasized the value of a constitution that united strength against foreign danger with security against internal corruption.[14] Madison could not subscribe completely to Montesquieu's endorsement of the "confederate republic." It smacked too much of the Articles of Confederation. But at least here was a hint of the possibility of a better organized "extensive republic." However, if Montesquieu was virtually silent on the constitution, or central principles of the "extensive republic," Hume spoke directly to the key questions that Madison raised. What were the operational mechanisms and explanatory ideas which might be applicable to the republican dilemma? How, in brief, could one reconcile republicanism and large size, popular government and factional danger?

In the "Idea of a Perfect Commonwealth," Hume had branded as a "falsehood" the "common opinion" "that no large state, such as France or Great Britain, could ever be modelled into a commonwealth, but that such a form of government can only take place in a city or small territory." "Though it is more difficult to form a republican government

31

in an *extensive* country than in a city, there is more facility when once it is formed, of preserving it steady and uniform, without tumult and faction." This would be the case, Hume argued, if indirect elections would be used and would take place in thousands of separate election districts. These techniques would refine popular passion without repudiating popular elections. The multiplicity of competing interests in such a system would operate to neutralize faction. In this way popular government and just government might be reconciled.[15]

Madison undoubtedly perceived the significance of these "luminous truths" in Montesquieu and in Hume because of his own devotion to religious liberty. This devotion was a central value in Madison's philosophical orientation, and it indicated his broadening of traditional republican commitments to liberty. It enabled him to see that the principle of multiplicity of sects that operated to ensure religious liberty might also operate (as the multiplicity of political, economic, and social interests) to ensure civil freedom. Human intelligence could perceive that religious uniformity was not essential to peace and order but might militate against them; that, indeed, religious diversity might advance freedom without interfering with civil decorum and harmony. Furthermore, human will could act to separate church and state and to guard against state action infringing on the rights of conscience. Thus, Madison's religious convictions carried over into the political arena. He could easily sympathize with Hume's argument that the wit and will of man could devise a new commonwealth "in some distant part of the world," a commonwealth which would reduce "theory to practice" and, in so doing, improve on "the common botched and inaccurate governments" of the moment.[16]

Not all the Federalists possessed Madison's faith or shared his vision. Adams, who was not at the Constitutional Convention, and Hamilton, who was, did not. They were not convinced that what Madison called an "extensive republic" was indeed feasible. According to Douglass Adair: "To both Adams and Hamilton history proved (so they believed) that sooner or later the American people would have to return to a system of mixed or limited monarchy—so great was the size of the country, so diverse were the interests to be reconciled that no other system could be adequate in securing both liberty and justice." [17] This may be an overstatement. We may challenge the contention that these monarchical views were fundamental and permanent convictions. Nonetheless, it is clear that both Adams and Hamilton were partial to key features of the mixed and balanced British system. They favored a strong central government; a strong executive whose monarch-like powers and prerogatives were to be employed on behalf of the common good of the nation; a lord-like Senate representing the rich, powerful and permanent interests of the realm; and, of course, a popular assembly.

If Adams and Hamilton thought that a strongly centralized government was necessary in 1787 to resolve the republican dilemma, the anti-Federalists were also pessimistic about an "extensive republic," albeit for different reasons. Patrick Henry, for example, exclaimed in the Virginia Ratifying Convention on June 9, 1788, "that one government cannot reign over so extensive a country as this is, without absolute despotism." Henry's view, as Douglass Adair has noted, was presumably based upon a "political axiom" scientifically confirmed—so Henry believed—by history. Henry's view was commonly shared by other anti-Federalists.[18]

"At the center of the theoretical expression of Anti-Federalist opposition to increased centralization of power in the national government," Cecelia M. Kenyon perceptively observes, "was the belief that republican government was possible only for a relatively small territory and a relatively small and homogeneous population...." "The fundamental issue over which Federalists and Anti-Federalists split was the question whether republican government could be extended to embrace a nation, or whether it must be limited to the comparatively small political and geographical units which the separate American states then constituted." [19]

Hints in Montesquieu and Hume had suggested a way out of the republican dilemma of trying to reconcile popular government and large size. But the momentous political task of translating theoretical hints into practical reality remained. Such a task, however, would not be successfully performed until the political theorist faced up to the realities of human behavior in politics, for—as Madison clearly saw—the republican dilemma involved not only large size but also the nature of man.

III

Madison held that freedom, an inalienable right, was man's natural condition. By "natural" and "inalienable," Madison understood what most advocates of a natural rights philosophy meant by these terms. Freedom was "natural" in the sense that the ability to be, think, and act was part of man's endowment as a whole, sane, normal, human personality. Freedom was "inalienable" in the sense that man ceased to be whole or human if freedom was taken away from him. Freedom, moreover, was intimately related to reason, and right reason led man to appreciate the value of a constitutional political order. The ability to be was the ability to live and to enjoy life. The ability to think and act was the ability to protect life more securely, to expand liberty more generously, to safeguard property more adequately, to ensure conscience more liberally, and to advance happiness more easily.

The sophisticated philosopher, the modern psychologist, and the empirical political theorist may throw up their hands in disgust at Madison's abstractions, methods, and axioms. The statesman, however, will find in Madison insights of prescriptive validity. In Madison's writings there was little philosophical analysis of the notion of freedom. He was less concerned with the scientific or metaphysical basis of the concept than with a view of freedom consonant with his understanding of the republican dilemma. The natural right to freedom was vital and enduring. It does not require a scientific public opinion poll or a controlled laboratory experiment to demonstrate that this view was held by republican men and influenced men like Madison to bring political reality into a more harmonious relationship with both the strengths and weaknesses of human nature. Madison was thus less concerned with the more precise definition and scientific proof of freedom as a natural right than with freedom's consequences for republican politics.

The most important consequence of freedom was human diversity—diversity in opinion, passion, talent, and interest. A second consequence was man's pursuit of his interests. A third consequence was man's use of power to gain his ends. Theoretically, these consequences were ethically neutral. Practically, however, it could not be expected that man's reason—as it could lead him to notions of justice and the common good—would always guide his pursuits. Diversity, self-interest, the use of power—these, then, were the primary consequences of the acceptance of freedom. This acceptance was clearly related to, and made politically inevitable by, Madison's normative commitment to a republican ideology.[20]

The secondary consequences of freedom were no less important. On the one hand, freedom provided opportunities for men's vices, particularly for factional damage to republican society; on the other, opportunities for virtue and the good republican life. Both vice and virtue were inconceivable without freedom. Unlike Calvin, Madison could not attribute vice to man and virtue to God. Man possessed the ability to do both good and evil, to be just and unjust. Hence, the age-old dilemma of freedom became a republican dilemma for Madison.[21]

This view of human behavior in a free society thus shaped the task of the republican theorist, the reconciliation of the conflicting consequences of freedom. Madison's way out of this dilemma was to insist that man's inclination to vice makes republicanism necessary, whereas his capacity for virtue makes republicanism possible. Man's ability to think and act could contrive a governmental system, ultimately founded on man's virtue, which would control faction. And if man's vices could not be eliminated, they might be controlled or even turned to republican advantage. The multiplicity of factional interests might make it extremely difficult for any single factional interest to gain and wield power. Madison's conception of the nature of man thus highlighted the two sides of the republican problem in a large state. How could one strengthen or maximize virtue and the good republican life? How could one control or utilize vice?

In Number 10 *Federalist,* Madison argued that the "latent causes of faction are . . . sown in the very nature of man."

A faction was a "number of citizens, whether amounting to a majority or minority of the whole, who are united and actuated by some common impulse of passion, or of interest, adverse to the rights of other citizens, or to the permanent and aggregate interests of the community." Repeatedly, in Madison's writings, men are revealed in part as passionate, fallible, shortsighted, unjust, ambitious, fickle, quarrelsome, opinionated, depraved, capricious, wicked, foolish, avaricious, and vain. If, then, the good republican life must rest on virtue, as almost everyone from Aristotle through Machiavelli agreed, the prospects for republicanism were gloomy. Because of their nature, Madison maintained, men have a zeal for religious, economic, governmental, and other opinions. They have an inclination to attach themselves to different, ambitious, and interesting leaders. Such zealousness reveals mankind's propensity "to fall into mutual animosities." Sometimes the animosity is based on fact, sometimes on fancy; sometimes on deep-seated differences, sometimes on frivolous distinctions.[22]

"But the most common and durable source of factions has been the various and unequal distribution of property. Those who hold and those who are without property have ever formed distinct interests in society. Those who are creditors, and those who are debtors, fall under a like discrimination. A landed interest, a manufacturing interest, a mercantile interest, a monied interest, with many lesser interests, grow up of necessity in civilized nations, and divide them into different classes, actuated by different sentiments and views."[23]

Because faction is rooted in human nature, it cannot be wished out of existence. Government, including republican government, is a reflection of that same human nature in which faction is rooted. Madison does not dodge the problem of the relationship of faction to government but states candidly that the "regulation of these various and interfering interests forms the principal task of modern legislation, and involves the spirit of party and faction in the necessary and ordinary operations of the government."[24]

A partisan and factional struggle for power thus seemed inevitable. The struggle became even more ominous when one noted that most of man's evil qualities became accentuated in the mass—and the larger the mass the worse the defects.

Unhappily, religion and conscience did not provide adequate restraints on the individual and certainly not on men in the mass. Nor could one depend on the individual or popular conviction that honesty is the best policy, or on the assumption that character will adequately check injustice. Furthermore, if ordinary citizens were not angels or philosopher-kings, neither were their elected representatives. Enlightened statesmen were rare. Among elected representatives, ambition and personal interest were more prevalent than desire for the public good. Consequently, legislative bodies were often unstable, unjust, contentious, confused, corrupt, incompetent, capricious, pernicious, intemperate, passionate, ignorant, and self-interested.[25]

The primary danger was that faction sought power and dominance and, at first glance, there did not appear to be sufficient virtue, intelligence, and will either in the electorate or in legislative bodies to prevent abuse of power or injustice. There existed no "Neutral Sovereign" to maintain justice among the contending interests and to advance the "permanent and aggregate interests of the community." This point is highly significant. It meant that Madison rejected the views of older republicans such as Machiavelli and even of "democratic" theorists such as Rousseau. These men had maintained that there is, initially, need for a "Legislator" or "Dictator" or "Wise Lawgiver"—a Solon as of old—to provide the people with the wise constitution and laws which will enable them to maintain republican government. Madison's rejection of this view meant that one could not rely upon a disinterested Lawgiver to establish a republican constitution. One could not count upon a "General Will" to advance the permanent and aggregate interests of the community. Nor could one depend upon a Neutral Sovereign to cope with the evil of faction. Furthermore, one could not look to a disinterested monarch or an aristocracy to maintain a neutral position above the battle or to dispense justice evenhandedly. The struggle of interests was not absent from monarchy or aristocracy, even though in these forms the struggle might be more stringently regulated. Such regulation, however, did not guarantee against abuse of power. Indeed: "In monarchies the interests and happiness of all may be sacrificed to the caprice and passions of a despot. In aristocracies, the rights and welfare of the many may be sacrificed to the pride and cupidity of the few." [26]

The struggle of interests presented a particular problem for republics. In a republic more men and interests had a rightful share in government and a greater assurance of liberty. Yet in the same republic, faction had a greater opportunity to shape public policy. Superficially, the republican outlook was not bright. Conflicts seemed unavoidable. One could not expect to find the "same interests" and the "same feelings" in all. No "society ever did or can consist of so homogeneous a mass of citizens." There did not exist a "Utopia exhibiting a perfect homogeneousness of interests, opinions and feelings." The population would inevitably increase, and this would mean an increase in "the proportion of those who will labour under all the hardships of life, and secretly sigh for a more equal distribution of its blessings." The "equal laws of suffrage" would strengthen the power of the many poor. Consequently, "agrarian attempts" and "leveling" constituted a "future danger." Moreover, as such "leveling" presented the future threat of the proletarian majority against the more prosperous minority, so actual or potential plutocratic elements would not hesitate to pervert the machinery of republican government to their own ends. [27]

If these are the consequences that flow from a realistic acceptance of human nature, then the prospects for republican government do, indeed, appear hopeless. But this is only half of Madison's view of the nature of man. The cynic might say that republicanism is necessary but hopeless—or hopeless but necessary. But Madison was no cynic; rather he was a responsible and dedicated republican statesman. He would push the argument a step farther. To understand Madison's conclusion that man's vices make republicanism necessary we must, therefore, consider his conviction, too frequently overlooked, that man's virtues make republicanism possible. Only in combination do the two conclusions make sense for the republican statesman.

Madison insisted that there were redeeming qualities in human nature which brightened the prospects for republican government. Diversity, self-interest, and power might serve to

counter as well as to facilitate faction. Even a partial examination of how these redeeming factors operate may make
clear why Madison was a more creative republican thinker
than Machiavelli, why he rejected the absolutism of Hobbes,
and why he deserted Hamilton and the Federalist party.
Madison refused to accept Machiavelli's great man theory as
a justification for the achievement of a strong, united, and
ultimately republican nation. He would not, with Hobbes,
posit the absolutism of Leviathan—an all-powerful state—as
the price to be paid for self-preservation and civilization. And
he would not abide by the aristocratic, plutocratic, and cen-
tralizing policy of Hamiltonian federalism when it appeared
to him that such a policy, despite its dedication to national
credit, confidence, and strength, ran counter to what Madison
considered to be the interest of the people and their republican rights.[28]

What, then, are the redeeming qualities in human nature
which brighten the prospects of republicanism? In Number
55 *Federalist,* Madison declared:

> As there is a degree of depravity in mankind which
> requires a certain degree of circumspection and distrust, so
> there are other qualities in human nature which justify a
> certain portion of esteem and confidence. Republican gov-
> ernment presupposes the existence of these qualities in a
> higher degree than any other form. Were the pictures
> which have been drawn by the political jealousy of some
> among us faithful likenesses of the human character, the
> inference would be, that there is not sufficient virtue
> among men for self-government; and that nothing less than
> the chains of despotism can restrain them from destroying
> and devouring one another.[29]

In this fashion, perhaps unconsciously, Madison wrote
off Hobbes. So he would also write off Hamilton, by insisting
upon a broader base for society than Hamilton's rich and
wellborn. So, too, he would later scoff at the notion that even
Washington could have become a Machiavellian leader or
dictator. Neither Washington's character nor the sense of the
American people supported such suspicions.[30]

Sufficient virtue—this was one redeeming quality. Another was intelligence. In defending the powers of Congress in

the Virginia Ratifying Convention, Madison joined the two, virtue and intelligence, in a holy republican union. He argued that he did not "place unlimited confidence" in the people's representatives "and expect nothing but the most exalted integrity and sublime virtue." Rather, one must operate on the "great republican principle" that "the people will have virtue and intelligence to select men of virtue and wisdom." If one rejected this principle, he declared, then one was indeed in a wretched situation." "No theoretical checks, no form of government, can render us secure." [31]

Sufficient virtue and sufficient intelligence—these must be taken into account along with vice and stupidity. However, still other redeeming qualities in man—duty, gratitude, and ambition—could be joined with self-interest and power to counteract man's sinful and factional predisposition. In Number 57 *Federalist*, Madison pointed out that such qualities in the people's representatives might support one's qualified confidence in elected representatives. Here Madison was replying to the charge that the members of the House of Representatives would have little sympathy for the mass of the people and would sacrifice the many to the few.

"Duty, gratitude, ambition itself, are the chords by which they will be bound to fidelity and sympathy with the great mass of the people. It is possible that these may all be insufficient to control the caprice and wickedness of man. But are they not all that government will admit and that human prudence can devise." [32]

Actually, as Madison himself believed, human prudence could devise in the theory of the "extensive republic" certain "auxiliary precautions" which could effectively explain how one might control the effects of factional wickedness. This theory, however, would accept the reality of diversity, self-interest, and power, and it would seek to maximize popular virtue and civic responsibility.

Lying back of Madison's qualified confidence in man's virtue, intelligence, and goodwill was his trust in the common sense of the people. This confidence was supported by his almost religious conviction of the triumph of reason and freedom. Additional support for trust in the people was his faith in education as a means of popular enlightenment. This trust, conviction, and faith in alliance with certain "auxiliary precautions" made republicanism possible. In this way popular rule in an "extensive republic" might be reconciled with individual rights, majority rule with the common good, central authority with local liberty, and order with freedom. It is here that one encounters the less familiar Madison. Here is the optimistic, hopeful, confident *philosophe.* Here is the broadly philosophic faith which supports that "honorable determination which animates every votary of freedom, to rest all our political experiments on the capacity of mankind for self-government." Here is the nourishment for Madison's belief that the "cool and deliberate sense of the community" ought to and will prevail.[33]

Madison's view of human nature was a tough-minded view of *man as he is.* He is free by nature. He differs from his fellows in physical and mental abilities, interests, and opinions. He is egoistically concerned with the pursuit of his own diversely motivated interests. He is inclined to use power to secure his own advantage in this world. He can be vicious or virtuous, ignorant or enlightened, apathetic or energetic, selfish or altruistic. This view was modified by Madison's recognition of *man as he can be.* He can be either a virtuous, educated, and competent citizen of a republic triumphant over faction, or an evil, ignorant, incompetent lout who has, by succumbing to passion, faction, and apathy, corrupted the republic and the liberties that free men might have enjoyed in a more perfect union. Finally, Madison's view of man was sustained by a deep-seated faith in *man as he ought to be.* He ought to be virtuous, intelligent, freedom-loving, self-respecting, vigilant, and independent. He ought to be capable of pursuing the public good and maintaining private rights, competent enough to sustain popular rule, able to conduct the affairs of a limited, responsible, representative government. These three perspectives overlap. The overlap suggests that Madison would work out a political theory which would call attention to the importance of feasible programs of action, designed in the light of the limitations and possibilities of empirical reality, to advance the central purposes of his republican orientation. This theory would be guided by inspiring normative goals but would be tempered by the limitations of political life. The stress would not be on either political utopia or political cynicism, but on feasible programs of action.

IV

The problem of harmonizing the claims of republican ideology, men's egoistic pursuit of diverse interests, and workable republican government in a large country was a continuing task throughout Madison's life. It made him concerned about Shays' Rebellion, which upset many in the year before the writing of the new Constitution in 1787. It disturbed him at the time of Hamilton's efforts in the 1790s to put his (Hamilton's) "stake in society" theory into effect. It alarmed him during the reign of political terror under the Alien and Sedition Acts (1798-1800). And it was still to frighten him during the significant sectional controversy in the late 1820s and early 1830s. At this time the tariff was the key issue, slavery lurked in the background of political debate, and nullification and secession were the Southern extremist's ultimate weapons of defense. In dealing with these issues Madison sometimes tended to make the lines separating political heaven and hell too sharp. He exaggerated deviations from the true republican faith. He overemphasized the evil qualities of man's nature which lay behind these deviations. This same duty to "write large" also led him to stress man's virtue, intelligence, and goodwill, which heartened those who sought to maintain the Republic.[34]

Paradoxically, the total effect is a more realistic view of man which, fortunately, does not hold that all men are necessarily well integrated or even that well-integrated men can always be relied upon. Madison seems to be telling us that there need only be trust in certain men who are capable of sound, rational action in a calmer, steadier, healthier environment in which most men might have an emotional as well as a rational confidence. In such an environment republican leadership could bring to decision, via reasonable compromise, issues affecting the nation.

In this appraisal I have tried to correct the opinion that Madison was hostile to popular rule and was sympathetic to a plutocratic defense of the status quo. A belief in democracy does not imply a belief that man is innately good and without sin. Nor does a belief in democracy require one to hold that all popular actions are just. Madison simply sought to protect man against unjust man, group against unjust group. He would stand on the side of justice, as he understood it, against whatever individual or group was opposed to the permanent and aggregate interest of the community. He would stand against factional majorities or minorities, whether unpopular or popular, whether state or sectional or national. He would always defend "liberty against power and power against licentiousness." [35]

Madison drew selectively from a number of different traditions in working out his view on human behavior in politics. His indebtedness to the classical, the Christian, the Natural Law, the Enlightenment, and the British Whig traditions is noticeable. The blending of all these traditions was, however, strongly conditioned by the favorable environment of America. The blend, moreover, had already found substantial expression in the American Revolutionary view of man. In the classical tradition, Madison held that man was a free, a rational, and an ethical creature who through effort and education could rear a societal structure capable of maintaining constitutional government. The Calvinistic-Christian interpretation of man, on the one hand, emphasized the impossibility of sinful man's achieving the good life by his own efforts; but, on the other, it conceded both the sense of republican rule for sinful man and the possibility that man's limited reason, love of liberty, and civic effort might enable him to maintain a happy republican polity. The Natural Law tradition emphasized man's natural rights, reasonableness, and sociableness. It held out the possibility of safeguarding basic rights through man's conscious will and deliberate effort. Men could erect a popular government which could protect life, liberty, conscience, property, happiness, and safety. The Enlightenment also encouraged those who looked ahead to the end of intellectual, political, and social tyranny. It stimulated those who felt that through education and constitutional government humanity would progress toward fuller realization. Madison, then, was not only a tough-minded, hardheaded, extremely able practical politician with both feet planted squarely in the realities of life. He was also a son of the Enlightenment, albeit a less blindly optimistic offspring than some.[36]

Yet despite his varied intellectual heritage, Madison remained an American Whig who had inherited from his British cousins not only a British love of liberty but also a British trust in the rule of law, representative institutions, constitutional government, and above all a superb pragmatic common sense. It was this pragmatic common sense that saved him from a temptation to assume that his psychological axioms held for all men everywhere. Madison did, of course, hold that all men were diversely motivated, egoistic, and power-oriented. However, these were fundamental universal qualities and did not require that Greek man, modern European man, and American man would be alike in all respects. Indeed, man's very diversity denied this possibility. Madison, a good student of both Aristotle and Montesquieu, appreciated that both education and environment could alter the secondary manifestations of man's nature. If this were not the case, there could be no progress toward greater political, intellectual, and religious freedom. Madison's common sense, as well as his wide reading in history, told him that there were indeed secondary differences between Americans and Britishers and between Anglo-Saxons and Greeks. The American Revolution, by fostering the spirit of nationalism, did as much as anything to make Madison see the unique possibilities of the American in the New World.

Madison thus maintained that man's complex nature makes republicanism both feasible and imperative. But what were the other necessary conditions for its survival in a large country? What else was required to avert either horn of the republican dilemma—a despotic empire or popular corruption?

CHAPTER 3

Nationalism and the
State of Disunion

> *"A weak constitution must necessarily terminate in disso-*
> *lution, for want of proper powers, or the usurpation of powers,*
> *requisite for the public safety."*
>
> —*The Federalist*, Number 20
>
> *"Government which relies on thirteen independent sover-*
> *eignties, for the means of its existence, is a solecism in theory,*
> *and a mere nullity in practice."*
>
> — 5 *Writings* 138 (1788)
> (Speech in Virginia Ratifying Convention)

I

Did the new nation face equally unacceptable alternatives: either a despotic empire strong enough to hold the
far-flung American states together or a weak confederation
composed of popular but corrupt states? Madison was unhappy about these alternatives. He favored a strong but free
union; he supported popular but just government. But could
he have his cake and eat it too? When he sought guidance
from the past to cope with the republican dilemma which his
republican ideology and the facts of life created, he got
precious little help. On the question, how to combine liberty
and large size, past history and theory provided little illumination. Initially, a candid understanding of human nature and
behavior did little to encourage hopes for a satisfactory solution of the dilemma. Diversity, self-interest, and the use of
power manifested themselves in factional activities which produced the danger of disunion and injustice. A little hope,
however, was held out by the other side of man's nature—his
virtue, intelligence, and goodwill. These, at least, suggested

45

more sanguine possibilities for just republican government in a large state.

But could virtue, intelligence, and goodwill alone cope with the problems of disunion, large size, faction, and anti-republicanism? These, as we have previously noted, were the four major difficulties that faced the new nation and obstructed the achievement of the more nearly perfect union. In this chapter I will focus on the problem of disunion as it emerged as a central problem in the 1780s and, then, later in the 1820s and 1830s. I shall concentrate primarily on Madison's diagnosis of the problem, briefly sketch his prognosis (which was to influence, and be altered by, the delegates to the Philadelphia Convention), and appraise the continuing validity of his analysis.

Madison's diagnosis of disunion—to be discussed in this chapter—suggests the need for a new concept of strengthened federal union with a federal government capable of operating directly on the individuals who compose the states of the union. Chapter 4, "The New Federalism," Part II, illustrates how Madison defends authoritatively the operative principles of a federal republic able to deal with the difficulty of large size without sacrificing liberty or autonomy for the people and component states of the new federal nation. These principles fall short of the more nationalistic ideas he had originally favored as essential in order to cope with disunion; but, as a prudent statesman, he would accept and defend the Compromise of 1787.

In Chapter 5, "Faction and the Extensive Republic," I will indicate at greater length how Madison's theory of the extensive republic explains how the adverse effects of faction might be controlled. This chapter will thus focus on the explanatory empirical theory which makes clear why the new operative principles of the federal republic—the prudential policies hammered out in the Philadelphia Convention—would indeed work to curb faction.

In Chapter 6, "The Anti-Republican Danger," I will be concerned primarily with Madison's response to Federalist policies in the 1790s, although I shall suggest the continuity of his concern as it manifested itself in the 1780s and was to guide his thinking in the 1820s and 1830s.

In general, in each of these chapters I will attempt to present Madison's diagnosis of and prognosis for the major difficulty involved, and then to appraise the continuing validity of his analysis.

In the twentieth century it was only in the post-World War II period—and largely as a result of our recognition of the problems facing new and developing nations, and of the civil rights movement in the United States—that Americans again became sensitized to the problem of disunion and the momentous task facing a nation as it seeks to integrate peoples, interests, and regions in a more nearly perfect union. Civil strife and civil war in the world call to mind again our own agonizing, traumatic experience from 1861-1865 and thus prepare us to understand the task of nation-building that faced the American nation in the still earlier period of 1776-1787. So, too, our continuing battle to integrate America's black citizens, and other ethnic minorities, forces us to remember previous discord on the issue of slavery, oppression, and national power and to appreciate anew the danger of disunion and the promise of a unity that combines strength and freedom, energy and justice.

Thus, we should now be better able to appraise the breakthrough in political theory that occurred with the emergence of the modern concept of federalism. We should be able to appreciate that prior to the birth of modern federalism in *The Federalist* few political theorists had tackled such problems as those pertaining to the proper relationship between the central government of a nation and its component states. What should be the character of such a republican federal union? What power should the central government have? What power the states? What should be the relationship of the central government to the people of the union? How could one reconcile liberty and empire, local self-government and central authority? If Americans were, indeed, born equal and free, as Alexis De Tocqueville in the nineteenth and Louis Hartz in the twentieth century have insisted, did this fortunate birth from a liberal British mother and an encouraging American father mean that Americans would necessarily stay free and equal in the absence of a more perfect union? Did the unique American environment and the liberal British political and economic tradition ensure as well as foster freedom? And if the answer to these two last questions is negative, what diagnosis of and prognosis for the state of disunion in the 1780s would, indeed, enhance a free and strong republican union? Here Madison's analysis becomes relevant—not only to the situation in the 1780s and, then, later in the 1820s and 1830s—but to our present discontents.

II

Madison diagnosed the ills of the union early in the 1780s. The fundamental cause of this weakness he attributed to the faulty "treaty" principle of union, upon which, he argued, the Articles of Confederation were based. Ultimately, on key matters each state of the union was a law unto itself. These states had come together for certain common purposes, but they were not willing to give up necessary sovereign powers to the central government of the union. The result was the continuation of the principle of *"imperia in imperio."* Each state within the union was sovereign, and on the crucial issues of raising money, regulating commerce, and handling such common matters as the western lands, a state would not give up its power to make the final decision to the central government. The states would—by arrangements resembling treaty relations between sovereign states, rather than by legislation of a true union government capable of operating directly on its citizens—handle matters as they arose. Such an arrangement would never, Madison argued, enable the United States of America to overcome the dangers of disunion. The pressing danger in the 1780s was the dissolution of the union and the concomitant abandonment of hopes for republican freedom. Usurpation—the seizure of power by anti-republican forces in the name of union, order, strength, justice—was also a danger, but less pressing at this time.

By the spring of 1787 Madison had systematized his indictment against the weakness, ineffectiveness, and disintegration of republican union under the government of the Articles of Confederation. He attributed the "Vices of the Political System of the United States" to eight causes: the states had failed to comply with the Union's request for funds;

they had encroached on federal authority; they had violated the laws of nations and confederation treaties; they had trespassed on each other's rights; the Union was unable to act in matters of common interest; the constitutions and laws of the states were not guarantees against internal violence; the laws of the confederacy lacked sanction and the government of the Confederation lacked coercive power; and, finally, the laws of the several states were unjust, too numerous, and too mutable.[1]

Madison's summary of the state of disunion in April 1787 was a masterfully succinct analysis of the defects of government, national and state, under the Articles of Confederation. It was the product of his own bitter experience in the Congress of the Confederation and of his own reflection upon the history of federal government. It told one a great deal about what a more perfect union should not be. It anticipated the positive government which was to emerge in the new constitution of 1787. Here, in embryo, was the new federalism.

This analysis, as I have suggested, was given concrete meaning by Madison's own experience as a representative from Virginia in the Congress of the Confederation. This analysis informed his key ideas in Philadelphia in 1787, aided him in defending the new union in *The Federalist* papers, and guided him in his attack on nullification and secession in the 1820s and 1830s. Although his views changed and matured through this period, his fundamental analysis of the weakness and danger of disunion remained the same.

Three of the major vices of the government under the Articles are illustrated by Madison's thought and action from 1780 through 1787. These demonstrate how Madison's theory of federal union evolved out of concrete political experience and was shaped by both history and theory. These three weaknesses were defective federal revenues, inadequate naional control of commerce, and conflicts over western lands. As Madison viewed the scene, he perceived these weaknesses and recognized that changes had to be made in America's political environment. Neither the fortunate American environment nor the liberal British inheritance would automatically remedy these weaknesses. And if changes were not made, republicanism would be drowned in a sea of disunion.

Defective fiscal policy was an early and continuing complaint. And always the defect was tied to the prospects of republican federal union. Money would win the war. Money would reconcile the army. Money would revivify confidence in the republic. Depreciated paper currency, state tender money laws, the absence of a national bank, unreliable sources of revenue, unjust economic arrangements, inadequate provision for the public debt—these threatened the Union. Without a sound fiscal policy, such evils would plague and eventually destroy the infant republic. Convulsions would break out in the army. States would dispute with each other. Creditors would seek a political connection with Great Britain as a hedge against internal instability. America would become embroiled in the wars and politics of Europe.[2]

A defective policy with regard to commerce was a second major point in Madison's early diagnosis of the less perfect union, and it, too, loomed large in Madison's analysis of the Articles' vices. Greater congressional power over commerce was necessary for a number of cogent reasons. It was needed to avoid foreign economic conflicts, involving the whole confederacy, although brought on by only one state of the Union. It was needed to counteract the restrictive trade practices of other countries. It was needed to increase America's commercial strength. It was needed to preserve the federal constitution. It was needed to prevent the dissolution of the confederacy.[3]

Another weakness involved the "Crown lands," America's western empire. Madison himself stated that the disposition of these lands "proved the most obstinate of the impediments to an earlier consummation of the plan of the federal Government." This "heartburning" matter merits special attention because it is so vitally related to the problem of the center and the circumference. Disagreement here, stemming from conflicting state claims and congressional weakness, made the operation of the Confederation more difficult. Union, as Madison recognized, could never become more nearly perfect as long as the states quarreled and Congress lacked the power to resolve their disputes in favor of the nation. Madison's concern for the surrender of Crown lands to Congress and his consistent regard for the right of navigation on the Mississippi reveal his recognition of the need for a strong government acting to secure its periphery. The central government's weakness on the frontier was a disturbing factor for a republic of large size.[4]

Lying back of these three major weaknesses, of course, were a number of other factors which "embarrassed the progress, and retarded the completion of the plan of Confederation." As Madison summarized them in 1835 in his subsequent sketch of the origins of the Constitutional Convention of 1787, they included the following: "the natural repugnance of the parties to a relinquishment of Power"; "a natural jealousy of its abuse in other hands than their own"; "the rule of suffrage among parties unequal in size, but equal in sovereignty"; "the ratio of Contributions in money and in troops, among parties, whose inequality in size did not correspond with that of their wealth, or of their military or free population"; and "the selection and definition of the powers, at once necessary to the federal head, and safe to the several members." [5]

This analysis of disunion provided the incentive for Madison's actions in seeking to secure a new charter of union for the infant American republic. This analysis indicates why he would push for the Annapolis Convention to assess the need for a more effective union, and why he would work so tirelessly on behalf of a new convention to obtain a new constitution. He had been deeply disturbed by the course of events he was personally experiencing as a practicing politician. Because he foresaw "the threatened danger of an abortive result to the great and perhaps last experiment" in "favour" of "free Government," he sought a way to rescue the Union and liberty from "impending disaster." Prudent guidance suggested the bold move that culminated in the Philadephia Convention.[6]

Madison's theoretical analysis in the spring of 1787—drawing as it did upon seven years of painful experience under the Articles of Confederation—informed his significant letters to Washington, Jefferson, and Randolph on the very eve of the Constitutional Convention. Here practical experience, a wide reading in history and past theory, and his own creative mind were at work in shaping the ingredients of a new republican, federal theory. Here diagnosis led naturally to prognosis. Here, too, the urgent need of a strong and effective union—so essential to free government—dictated the more nationalistic approach that characterized Madison's position immediately before and during the Philadelphia Convention. This analysis, we must remember, anticipated the so-called Randolph or Virginia Plan, which provided the initial frame for discussion of the new constitution.[7]

The danger of disunion dominated Madison's arguments in the Constitutional Convention. To respond to this danger, Madison again and again emphasized the need for "sufficient powers" in the "Common Government" and attacked the selfishness and narrowness of the states. Madison's cardinal fear was that of a union operating on the faulty principle of *"imperia in imperio,"* a principle which could only lead to the demise of republican government in America.[8]

The continuity of Madison's diagnosis of the danger of disunion is apparent in *The Federalist.* Much of his analysis appears in those historical numbers which most readers skip and which are often left out of abridged editions. From his study of "federal precedents," a study which he had made prior to the Philadelphia Convention, Madison had drawn the conclusion that a "weak constitution must necessarily terminate in dissolution, for want of proper powers, or the usurpation of powers requisite for the public safety." Of these two dangers, dissolution was the more threatening in the 1780s. Madison's historical studies "emphatically" illustrated "the tendency of federal bodies rather to anarchy among the members, than to tyranny in the head." Yet he recognized that a weak constitution might lead to usurpation. "Tyranny," he warned, "has perhaps oftener grown out of the assumption of power called for, on pressing exigencies, by a defective constitution, than out of the full exercise of the largest constitutional authorities." [9]

It was the wise course, the prudent course, to avoid the danger by strengthening a defective constitution before it was too late. This is why, as Madison had written to Jefferson, "the difficulties" and the "mortal diseases of the existing Constitution [of the Confederation]" challenged "the votaries of liberty [to make] every concession in favor of stable government not infringing fundamental principles, as the only security against an opposite extreme [i.e., usurpation or tyranny] of our present situation." [10]

Madison recognized that new governmental principles were needed to counter the "evil of imperia in imperio," which "seems to have been mortal to the antient Confederacies, and to be the disease of the modern." Here Madison was disturbed by the same republican dilemma of freedom and power: too much freedom for the states might result in a disruption of the union; too much power for the central government might lead to tyranny. "A *voluntary* observance of the federal law by all the members could never be hoped for. A *compulsive* one could evidently never be reduced to practice, and if it could, involved equal calamities to the innocent and the guilty, the necessity of a military force both obnoxious and dangerous, and in general a scene resembling much more a civil war than the administration of a regular government." Here it is important to stress that Madison's diagnosis underlined the connection between the danger of disunion and the danger to republicanism, a point too frequently overlooked by those who emphasize Madison's nationalism in 1787 at the expense of his republicanism. As he wrote to Jefferson, the "most steadfast friends of Republicanism" saw the tie between effective union and republican life and, consequently, must act accordingly. [11]

This same theoretical analysis guided Madison's arguments in the crucial Virginia Ratifying Convention. The real threat confronting American union was factionalism in the states, not the tyranny of the proposed central government. Such factionalism would continue to run rampant as long as the "treaty" principle of the Confederation prevailed. By this principle Madison meant that a "Government which relies on thirteen independent sovereignties, for the means of its existence, is a solecism in theory, and a mere nullity in practice." A central government needed energy, strength, and stability. "Governments destitute of energy will ever produce anarchy." A strong and vigorous government, he reminded those Virginia delegates with western ties, would also be better able to secure the right of navigation of the Mississippi. This, in turn, would enhance the property, strength, and security of the

Union and solidify the allegiance of the West to the Union. Throughout his argument Madison utilized the "lessons of history" to reinforce those Americans whose experiences suggested the need for a new experiment in republican and federal union.[12]

As the greatest act in Madison's political career opened with the cloud of disunion hanging ominously over the American scene, so the last years of his life came to a close with a similar cloud, shaped by the twin heresies of nullification and secession, threatening to deluge the land with many of the same evils Madison had earlier fought so valiantly against. These evils, Madison prophetically declared, involve a "rupture of the Union; a Southern confederacy; mutual enmity with the Northern; the most dreadful animosities and border wars, springing from the cause of slaves; rival alliances abroad, standing armies at home, to be supported by internal taxes; and federal Governments with powers of a more consolidating and monarchical tendency than the greatest jealousy has charged on the existing system." [13]

So Madison wrote on February 10, 1833—at least twenty-eight years before the Civil War!

Dissolution, Madison pointed out at the end of his career as he had at the beginning, would be "fatal to the hopes of liberty and humanity." Madison was vehemently opposed to the doctrines of nullification and secession because he saw more clearly than Calhoun and other defenders of the Southern cause that these doctrines were incompatible with a more nearly perfect union. The power of a state to nullify a federal law, the power of a state to secede from the federal union—these would admit the validity and legitimacy of a principle of union which Madison had so strongly condemned in the "Vices." This was the "treaty" principle, which held that the Union was, in the last analysis, an alliance of sovereign states, each of which possessed the power to dissolve the Union when a breach of the treaty establishing the alliance had occurred. The theory of nullification and secession would, in effect, cancel the attempt to secure a more perfect union. The nation would return to a condition not unlike that under which it had lived under the Articles of Confederation. Each state would again possess at least a temporary veto power over federal legislation. Unanimity would again be required for the orderly functioning of national law, even if an overwhelming majority of states could theoretically obligate a single state to withdraw its nullification of a national law. The more nearly perfect republican, federal union could not long survive if these doctrines were to prevail. This is why Madison so bitterly condemned them as spurious, heretical, and dangerous.[14]

Madison contended, perceptively, that it was "madness in the South to look for greater safety in disunion. It would be worse than jumping out of the Frying-pan into the fire; it would be jumping into the fire for fear of the Frying-pan." Nullification and secession were not the principles that would provide protection against either anarchy or tyranny. On the contrary, these principles militated against both individual liberty and state authority. They were not, in brief, the prudent alternative to a new republican, federal system.[15]

The absurd and dangerous consequences of Calhoun's logical, but imprudent, doctrine seem never to have been perceived by the rash advocates of nullification and secession. Few were alive in the 1830s who remembered the state of disunion in the 1780s. Madison in 1833 did perceive these consequences because he had been burned once before by the principle of unanimity under the Articles of Confederation. A lack of basic uniformity and the absence of fundamental concert had been vices of the Union under the Articles. They remained vices inherent in the doctrines of nullification and secession. "There cannot be," Madison insisted, "different laws in different states on subjects within the compact without subverting its fundamental principles, and rendering it as abortive in practice as it would be incongruous in theory." "In a word, the nullifying claims if reduced to practice, instead of being the conservative principle of the Constitution, would necessarily, and it be said obviously, be a deadly poison." [16]

The spirit of 1787 was vividly manifest in Madison's devastating attack on nullification in the 1830s. The nationalist of 1787 who had become a limited constructionist in the 1790s still relied upon his 1787 diagnosis of disunion to smite the dragon of nullification.

If one could not operate on the principle of the unanimity of states in 1787, one could not rely on the same principle in the 1820s and 1830s. And unanimity *within* states was equally impossible. If it were accepted *within* each state, such a state would be as paralyzed in its action as would the United States of America. The result would be anarchy *within* each state. If unanimity were not accepted, each state would have to operate within its sovereign area on the same principle of majority rule which Calhoun and his followers opposed for the government of the union. The result would be inadequate protection—following Calhoun's own logic—for the minorities within such a state. The anti-republican implications and consequences of Calhoun's political theory will be spelled out in more detail in Chapter 6. Here we need only note that Madison's understanding of the conditions of the more nearly perfect union enabled him to demolish the theory of nullification and secession even more ably than he had attacked the "treaty" principle of union of the Articles of Confederation.[17]

One final point remains to be made with regard to Madison's diagnosis of the danger of disunion in the 1820s and 1830s. This relates to the role of parties as associations capable of dividing or uniting the union. If Madison recognized the divisiveness of interests and the stupidity of the "treaty" concept of union both in 1787 and during the 1830s, he also appreciated the danger of sectional parties and the need for national concert in both periods. If divisive state interests worried him in 1787, divisive sectional interests alarmed him in the 1820s and the 1830s. Specifically, what Madison feared in 1820 was the division—because of the issue of extension of slavery—of the old Republican party that he and Jefferson had built. This might lead, he wrote to Monroe, to a "new state of parties founded on local instead of political distinctions." This could be dangerous to union since it might lead to sectional war.[18]

A few months earlier he had prophetically identified the issue which was to become so tragically real in 1860: "Parties under some denomination or other must always be expected in a Government as free as ours. When the individuals belonging to them are intermingled in every part of the whole Country, they strengthen the Union of the Whole, while they divide every part. Should a State of parties arise, founded on geographical boundaries and other Physical and permanent distinctions which happen to coincide with them, what is to control those great repulsive Masses from awful shocks against each other?" [19] This fear of a rupture of the Union thus remained an enduring point in Madison's diagnosis of disunion. If factional interests in the states were a prime fear in 1787, factional parties in the nation were a major danger in the 1820s and 1830s.

III

First, diagnosis; then, remedy. This was Madison's method as a theoretician. His diagnosis of the state of disunion under the Articles of Confederation had uncovered the weaknesses of federal union. It now remained to remedy those weaknesses. The remedy must give the central government necessary strength, authority, energy, stability, confidence, and respect. Yet it must also preserve all the people's republican liberties, and their control over their local affairs. In deciding how to strike this balance, Madison did not hesitate to opt for a strong nationalism—a strengthened union operating directly on the people and capable of maintaining its own integrity and republican justice.

Madison's letters to Washington, Jefferson, and Randolph before the Philadelphia Convention stressed three crucial points. First, it was necessary, positively, to equip the government of the union with sufficient substantive, legal, and coercive powers. Such powers must operate on the people directly. Only such powers could guard against the great danger of disunion and ensure action in matters of common interest. Second, it was necessary, negatively, to protect the union's own integrity, in both the domestic and foreign fields, against selfish state interests which threatened the "aggregate interests of the community." Third, it was necessary to ensure stable, orderly, just republican government in the several states by limiting the power of the states and hence the power of faction within the states.[20]

The sweeping nationalism of these ideas informed the so-called Randolph or Virginia Plan, which provided the initial basis for discussion of the new constitution.

The sweeping nationalism that Madison brought to the Convention is still startling today. Although it is obvious that prior to the Convention he was still searching for specific theoretical weapons with which to crush the monster of disunion, the general drift of his thinking is clear. The new federal union must be based upon a principle different from the "treaty" principle. It must be based on the sovereign people of the states and be capable of operating directly upon individuals. Unanimity as a basis for action, even on crucial matters, must give way to majority decision. National uniformity and concert were to be obtained by firmly establishing the principle of due national supremacy in all branches of the new government. The central government was to acquire the requisite energy and stability by achieving significant powers over such vital matters as taxation and commerce. Such power must be unimpeded by the ability of the states to hold back on the raising of revenue or to obstruct uniform commercial policies. Furthermore, the states were to be held in line by other devices. Significantly, these included such strongly nationalistic proposals as federal coercion, a federal veto over interfering state legislatures, as well as prohibition of a number of state actions.

However, not all aspects of Madison's embryonic federal theory were politically feasible. The federal theory that finally emerged from the Convention was shorn of several key features to which Madison had been originally strongly committed. Here, an examination of the successes and failures of Madison's remedies is highly instructive because it indicates concretely how theory is shaped by the limitations and possibilities of political reality.

Let me start with Madison's advocacy of the idea of federal coercion of the states. This idea goes back to his efforts, under the government of the Articles of Confederation, to get the states to furnish their monetary quotas for the support of the central government. Experience had indicated that a union based upon voluntary compliance would fail. Congress, therefore, must have coercive powers or an equally effective alternative. Nevertheless, despite his advocacy of these ideas between 1781 and 1787, Madison remained unhappy about the necessity for coercion used directly against the state governments. He continued to search for alternative solutions.[21]

One such alternative was direct operation of the government upon the people. In 1787 Madison explicitly repudiated the "treaty" theory of union, which made the union a mere league or friendship pact, and explicitly advocated a union based upon the people. The people were to be represented in the central government according to free population and/or monetary contributions to the new central government. Madison wanted to get as far as possible from the principle of equality of states in the new central government. This principle he associated with the unanimity principle of the Articles of Confederation, which permitted the least populous and least generous states to frustrate the will of the overwhelming majority. Hence, before and during the Convention, Madison recommended that the new government be able to operate directly on the people. They might be taxed directly. Necessary federal laws would affect them directly.[22]

Yet Madison was not entirely satisfied with this alternative. It might be a necessary condition of the more nearly perfect union but it was not a sufficient condition. Thus he continued to harbor the older belief that federal coercion of states, although undesirable and unworkable, was still essential. His reluctance to part with this idea was intellectually agonizing. The idea of coercion thus turned up in the Virginia Plan. Resolution Number 6 of the Virginia Plan suggests that Madison, the primary author of the plan, believed that the National Legislature might have to "call forth the force of the Union against any member of the Union failing to fulfill its duty. . . ." Madison's uncertainty about coercion is again indicated by his change of mind in the Convention. There he himself suggested that the Convention drop the coercion clause. As he told Jefferson later, coercion was simply not feasible. It was more sensible to rely upon "the alternative of a Government which instead of operating on the States, should operate without their intervention on the individuals composing them. . . ." [23]

Nevertheless, Madison still sought other alternatives which would operate to keep the states in their proper places. One of the most important of these was the notion of a "federal negative," or national veto, on the acts of the states. Before journeying to Philadelphia, Madison had called for a "negative *in all cases* whatsoever on the legislative acts of the States" which invade the legitimate jurisdiction of the nation. This became in the Virginia Plan the power "to negative all laws passed by the several States contravening in the opinion of the National Legislature the articles of Union." Such a negative, Madison had written before the Convention, "appears to me to be absolutely necessary, and to be the least possible encroachment on the State jurisdictions." Such a "negative" Madison had compared to the British king's prerogative.[24]

In the Philadelphia Convention, Madison battled valiantly for this veto which, he argued, *"would render the use of force unnecessary."* It *"must extend to all cases."* Only this principle could "control the centrifugal tendency of the States; which, without it, will continually fly out of their proper orbits and destroy the order and harmony of the political system." Such a veto, moreover, was preferable to subsequent repeal by the "General Legislature" or to invalidation by state or national tribunals. It was better to prevent a fire than to put it out after it had occurred.[25]

However, the Convention was not convinced by Madison's pleadings. Only with the greatest reluctance, and after several adverse votes, did Madison abandon his fight for a "federal negative," which he continued for some time to feel was the heart of any plan to deal with disunion. Madison's persistent and prophetic fear was that in the absence of a "federal negative" the "due supremacy" of the nation might be established only by a recourse to arms. He did recognize the argument "that the Judicial authority, under our new system, will keep the states within their proper bounds, and supply the place of a negative on their laws." But he was, at this time, by no means convinced of the cogency of this argument. A "State which would violate the Legislative rights of the Union," he wrote to Jefferson, "would not be very ready to obey a Judicial decree in support of them." State disobedience would then make a "recurrence to force" "necessary," and this was "an evil which the new Constitution meant to exclude as far as possible." [26]

When the "negative" was "finally rejected by a bare majority," Madison had to rely more heavily on the remaining operational features of his federal theory. Some of these features involved positive powers. Thus, before the Convention, Madison had in a letter to Washington urged a "national government" "armed with positive and compleat authority in all cases which require uniformity." He sought to establish the "due supremacy" of the union in those areas wherein the union must undoubtedly be supreme if the objectives of a more perfect union were to be achieved. The more important areas included the regulation of trade, the right to tax both exports and imports, and the fixing of the terms and forms of naturalization. This suggestion to Washington became transformed in the Virginia Plan into a "National Legislature . . . impowered . . . to legislate in all cases to which the separate states are incompetent, or in which the harmony of the United States may be interrupted by the exercise of individual legislation. . . ." This was, indeed, a broad and sweeping grant of power. This clause was clearly intended to provide a generous grant of power over commerce to Congress. Thus, in the Convention, Madison held that "the regulation of commerce was in its nature indivisible and ought to be wholly under one authority." Similarly, he urged the Convention to give Congress the power to grant charters of incorporation.[27]

In addition to these positive powers, Madison urged the adoption of a number of prohibitions on the actions of the separate states. Thus, he would prevent the states from taxing either imports or exports. He would prohibit *ex post facto* laws and interference by states with private contracts. These prohibitions were called for by his analysis in the "Vices." They were made necessary by the tendency of the states to ignore the common interest and private rights.[28]

A number of other Madisonian recommendations advanced in the spring of 1787 were also written into the Constitution. These, too, had been called for by his acute diagnosis in the "Vices." The national executive must be made truly independent of the will of the state legislatures. Otherwise, national supremacy was impossible. Judges must take an oath of fidelity to the United States as well as to their respective state constitutions. Judges must be obligated to uphold federal laws. Moreover, the people—not the state legislatures—must ratify the new constitution. Only in this way could the people composing the states of the nation have a fresh and clear opportunity to approve the new union.[29]

In general, Madison battled in the Convention for those features which would make the union strong and against those features which contributed to disunion, weakness, and ineffectiveness. Thus he unsuccessfully opposed equality of representation in the Senate, but he successfully argued against payment of Senators by the States. He successfully favored guaranteeing the tranquility of the states against internal as well as against external danger, and he successfully favored a stable Senate of long tenure. If one reads his speeches in the Convention, one cannot miss the emphasis upon strengthening the union in order to remedy the vices which he had outlined before the Convention.[30]

Madison's strong nationalism is also apparent in his position on the West and on the presidency. His concern for the West exemplifies his sensitivity to the problem of reconciling the center and the circumference. He favored treating the new states that might be admitted from the West equally with the older states. New states should not be handicapped in coming into the union. They should not be discriminated against. Although hostile to the principle of unanimity and representation under the Articles of Confederation, Madison did not want to make satellites or colonies out of the new states. The people in those states were to be treated on the same basis as the people in the original states. Only in this way would the states at the circumference be reassured. Only in this way would stable and orderly growth be possible. Only in this way could an extensive republic work.[31]

This same nationalistic concern for the union as a whole also emerges in Madison's conception of the President. He viewed the President as a national officer who would be "acting for and equally sympathising with every part of the United States." The President must act for the whole people or at least a true majority of them, in contrast to a majority of states.[32]

Madison's concern for due national supremacy carried him to a nationalistic pinnacle in 1787. He was a nationalist because he was concerned for that which pertained to the nation as a whole. This nationalism is revealed not only by those proposals—of federal coercion and federal veto—which he had originally favored and which were finally rejected by the Convention in favor of more politically feasible alternatives, but also by those proposals which he had opposed and which the Convention finally adopted. Thus he opposed proposals embodied in two of the major compromises of the Convention—equality of representation of states in the Senate and a prohibition against a national tax on exports. He vehemently opposed the first proposal because it gave the states a greater agency in the new government than he wanted them to have. He did not want the Senate to be representative of state governments. He wanted to move as far away as possible from a government of the union which gave the states an opportunity to frustrate the will of the nation. For similar nationalistic reasons, again in opposition to the proposal finally accepted, he supported a national tax on exports because this would give Congress the substantial power in the field of commerce that he believed the new nation must have if it were to survive and prosper.[33]

To make these points is to indicate again Madison's original strong nationalistic remedy for disunion. This emphasis, despite shifts in the 1790s in favor of limited construction, emerged again in his prognosis for the state of disunion in the 1820s and 1830s, as disunion here was brought on by the doctrines of nullification and secession. Again, Madison stressed the principle of due national supremacy and the need for acceptance of the principle of majority rule in the union. The principle of unanimity—whether in the government of the Articles of Confederation or in Calhoun's doctrine of the concurrent majority—could lead only to anarchy and impotence. The doctrine of the concurrent majority—linked as it was with nullification and secession—would give each state or major section of the nation the power to veto national action. Nullification gave to a state the power to set aside national laws; secession, the power to withdraw from the national union. And Madison made no effort to conceal his condemnation of these heretical doctrines.

"Nullification has the effect of putting powder under the Constitution and Union, and a match in the hand of every party to blow them up at pleasure." [34]

"The idea that a Constitution which has been so fruitful of blessings, and a Union admitted to be the only guardian of the peace, liberty and happiness of the people of the states comprising it, should be broken up and scattered to the winds . . . is more painful than words can express." [35]

Majority rule in the nation must be accepted as a cardinal principle of republican union. To reject it was to reject republicanism and to disrupt the union. The alternatives to majority rule would neither safeguard minority or individual rights nor preserve the union. Since there was no unanimity of interests within a state, and since each state would have to rely on majority rule in its own government, unless it were to succumb to individual anarchy or governmental impotence, the minority would not find within a state, and outside the union, the greater safety it sought. Madison insisted that abuses of power, stemming from the conflict of agricultural and manufacturing interests, would occur within a single state as well as within the union. If majority government in the union was improper, it was also improper as it operated within each state. The alternative to majority government was either non-republican government or anarchy. In brief, Madison contended that the doctrine of the concurrent majority— which was an attack on the majority principle as it operated in the government of the union—did not really solve the problem of protecting minorities against the conflict of interests or against majority decision at lower levels or against majority abuse of power. And, in addition, this doctrine was destructive of union.[36]

Within the framework of a union, based upon due national supremacy and operating on the principle of majority rule, action must be taken to accommodate diverse and conflicting interests, and thus heal the sectional breach. Such action must be taken before the extremists could gain control and jeopardize republican union. Here Madison relied not only on sound republican and nationalist theory—based on the concepts of a strong and just federal republic and a united and functioning Republican party—but also on a number of other key factors. Among these were the binding forces of patriotic sentiment, common religious denominations, mutual economic self-interest, and enlightened statesmanship. Such statesmanship involved more moderate Southern leadership, a realistic and honest understanding of the true causes of the South's distress, a sane reduction of the tariff, and an equitable sharing of necessary economic burdens.[37]

If relative success crowned Madison's efforts in 1787 in his struggle with the problem of disunion, the same was not true of his last great struggle in the 1820s and 1830s on behalf of union. Unfortunately, after Madison's death in 1836, his remarkable grasp of the issues was not shared by any statesman—North or South—who commanded the ability to translate Madison's diagnosis and prognosis into public policy. It remained for Lincoln, after civil war had broken out, to cherish Madison's advice that the union of the states be perpetuated.

IV

How do we appraise the historical and contemporary validity of Madison's analysis of the problem of disunion?

In the Philadelphia Convention, Madison's nationalism reached its flood tide. In one speech he had even argued, theoretically, that a unitary government was not necessarily incompatible with freedom or local self-government. Practically, however, he conceded that a federal government served sensibly to divide responsibility in serving the people's needs. Later in his life, when Robert Yates' notes on the proceedings of the Constitutional Convention were published, some critics hastily concluded that Madison had advocated a unitary, consolidated government. He had not. He had simply advanced a theoretical argument to drive home his immediate point: that in 1787 the state governments were the primary enemies of the more perfect union and that the central government was not to be feared. To some, however, Madison's argument sounded so heretical that it could only have been uttered in the secrecy of the Convention's sessions.[38]

This is misleading; for, later, Madison made a comparable argument publicly in several numbers of *The Federalist*.

Read closely, the alleged heretical statement in the Convention and the arguments in *The Federalist* are of the same pragmatic cloth. In Numbers 45 and 46 *Federalist*, Madison said in effect that the rivalry of nation and states for the allegiance of the people would be determined primarily by the ability of the nation or the states to do a satisfactory job for the people. This would determine the amplitude and shift of power. The pragmatic test of ethical and political success, not abstract notions of sovereignty, would be the proper guide in determining the respective powers of nation and states. If the job were well done, power and respect would be given to the just and efficient government, national or state. If the performance were unsatisfactory, these would not be forthcoming. This suggests, incidentally, why Madison's strong nationalism in the Convention was to ebb in the 1790s.[39]

It is also important to emphasize that if Madison's nationalism in 1787 was strong and unmistakable, so was his dedication to republican theory. For example, just as his subsequent opposition to the anti-republican character of the Alien and Sedition Acts and to so much of the Hamiltonian program was already implicit in his treatment of the eighth vice—injustice— of the Confederation, so too was his opposition to nullification and secession implicit in his treatment of vices two, five, and seven—which deal with the necessary power that is required in order to preserve a strong republican union.

Madison's strong nationalism, which I have argued was a direct response to his diagnosis of the problem of disunion, has led some observers to ask what his position was on the enumeration of the powers of the central government in 1787. In an early speech in the Philadelphia Convention on May 31, he declared "that he had brought with him into the Convention a strong bias in favor of enumeration and definition of the powers necessary to be exercised by the national Legislature; but had also brought doubts concerning its practicability. His wishes remained unaltered; but his doubts had become stronger. What his opinion might ultimately be he could not tell. But he should shrink from nothing which should be found essential to such a form of government as would provide for the safety, liberty and happiness of the community. This being the end of all our deliberations, all the necessary means for attaining it must, however reluctantly, be submitted to." [40]

Unquestionably, he favored a great and significant expansion and invigoration of the powers of the central government to enable it to cope with matters of common concern. He preferred to leave local matters to the states. He did not, however, favor a unitary or consolidated government which would obliterate all the powers of the states. A reasonable conclusion is that in the summer of 1787 Madison sought a stronger national government than the one adopted, but he had no intention of depriving the states of powers in matters not relevant to the national interest. In 1787 Madison apparently had not thought through the question of the specific extent of national power. Hence his position on the question is partly ambiguous. It is, however, clear that his nationalism of 1787 was as strong as—if not stronger than—that which we have historically associated with Hamilton and Marshall; and like that of these two men, Madison's nationalism of 1787 anticipated that of Theodore Roosevelt, Woodrow Wilson, and Franklin Roosevelt in the twentieth century.

What is clear is that Madison preferred to accept a constitution which was not ideal, rather than to hold out dogmatically and unsuccessfully for one which would have been more powerful.[41] This prudent disposition to compromise, which had already manifested itself in the Convention, became stronger after the Convention adjourned; and Madison was faced with the task of getting the new constitution adopted. Then, in response to these political realities, he would defend a document which was less national and more federal than he had originally hoped it would be. To convince opponents of an alleged all-powerful, consolidated government, he would emphasize both the limited powers of the central government and the abundant powers to be exercised by the varying states. Still later he would argue that the true meaning of the Constitution was to be found—not necessarily in the views of the architects of 1787 as they debated in the Philadelphia Convention—but in the sense of the ratifying conventions. This conviction would enable him later, when reaction to the Hamiltonian fiscal program and the Alien and Sedition Acts dictated a shift away from his strong nationalism of 1787, to emphasize a much more restricted view of the powers of the central government than he had held in the Convention.

Madison's theory of federal union unquestionably evolved in response to the political realities which strongly indicated the need to alleviate the fears of the anti-Federalists, those opposed to a stronger central government. However, it is hardly just to accuse Madison of deliberate dishonesty because his strong nationalism of 1787 was tempered by the heat of political feasibility in 1787 and 1788 and by the alleged anti-republican danger posed by Federalist policy in the 1790s. Madison never forgot that means must prudently be adapted to advance one's end. Consequently, if the "middle ground" solution of the spring and summer of 1787 was too nationalistic for the political temper of the times, a more moderate nationalism must be accepted. The object, however, remained the same: a new constitution that would remedy the state of disunion.

Later in his lifetime, as I have already indicated, the far-reaching nationalistic notions of the Virginia Plan were to lead to ugly accusations that the "design of the plan" "was to render the States nothing more than provinces of a great Government, to rear upon the ruins of the old Confederacy a Consolidated Government, one and indivisible." Madison's denial of this charge placed him in an uncomfortable position. He had to reject the false view that he sought a "Consolidated Government" without candidly admitting that his strong nationalism of 1787 did, indeed, call for a central government with more power than he was willing, in the 1790s and later, to concede it ought to possess. Madison was correct in stating that there is "certainly no ground" for imputing "consolidating views" to the authors of the Virginia Plan. He never sought a "Consolidated Government with unlimited powers." Yet he was somewhat disingenuous in maintaining that the Virginia Plan did not contemplate a "Government materially different from or more national than that" which emerged in 1787.[42] It was, however, entirely possible for Madison in 1787 to seek a very broad legislative discretion for the central government while still adhering to the conception of national powers specified and limited by the Constitution. The fact that he was later unwilling to admit the more generous powers he advocated for the central government and the more severe limitations he favored for state governments must be attributed to the human frailty that Madison, despite his unimpeachable integrity, was heir to as a son of Adam.

How helpful is Madison's analysis of disunion to an understanding of American federalism? How relevant is it to our present federal discontents? The faulty principle of the Articles of Confederation made the more nearly perfect union impossible because it denied the government of the Union requisite strength, energy, stability, confidence, and respect. Without these the nation could not survive. Without these a republic could not advance the ends of its citizens. Obviously, a significant step toward a solution was taken in 1789. Some of its strengths and weaknesses we will explore in a moment. Here it need only be noted that from 1787 to 1789, and then later in the midst of the nullification controversy, Madison never argued that the Union of the new constitution was perfect or that policies made under it were always wise and fair. Such thinking was utopian. Such a mentality was inconsistent with the fact that the Constitution and public policies made under it were based on mortal, fallible men living in a dynamic society. All vital interests must be preserved but not at the price of anarchy. Sectional interests must be respected but not at the cost of the sacrifice of republicanism. The new union was not perfect but it was immensely superior to a "purely consolidated" or a "purely federal" government.

An appraisal of Madison's analysis of vices and recommendations in 1787 reveals not only the perceptiveness of his grasp of modern federalism at its birth in his own day, but also a prophetic identification of the enduring problems of federal government. This analysis was deepened by—and becomes even more prophetic in the light of—his critique of the dangers of disunion in the theorists of nullification.

Largely following Madison's federal road map in 1787, most observers will agree, the nation took the right road. Madison had charted a course and indicated the dangers along the way. Some of the dangers were eliminated in 1787; others were brought under control; still others were at least clearly identified. Hence, Madison's diagnostic and prognostic contribution to federal theory must be understood in terms of

his illumination of enduring problems and of his recommendations for the handling of major difficulties. A brief examination of the vices Madison perceived in 1787, as some of them
were also illustrated by the dangerous heresy of nullification
in the 1820s and 1830s, will clarify this contribution.

Although the problem of an independent and reliable
source of revenue was temporarily solved for the central
government in 1787, the problem of an ample and effective
revenue remained to annoy a rich America during crisis periods like the Civil War. The problem of money became particularly disturbing as the demand for services provided by the
central government became louder and more intense. The
battle over the progressive income tax still had to be fought
more than a hundred years after the Constitutional Convention, to the end that the central government might be able to
collect equitably the funds it needed on behalf of national
responsibilities. And if the central government today has the
monies it needs, it cannot be denied that an independent and
reliable source of revenue is for most of the fifty states their
most pressing problem. Now, ironically, the national government is not at the mercy of funds tendered by the state
governments, but vice versa.

The self-interested encroachment of the states on federal
authority has also been a continuing problem, historically,
and remains—even if only in minor matters—a problem today. In matters of interstate and foreign commerce, taxation
of such federal instrumentalities as a national bank, and in
dealings with Indian tribes, it took a nationalist Supreme
Court, under Chief Justice Marshall, to establish Madison's
principle of due national supremacy. Again and again
throughout our history, states have invaded federal jurisdiction. The temptation to encroach seems to be an inherent
feature of any federal pattern which reserves to the states
ample powers to handle their own local affairs. The federal
system adopted in 1787 improved on the constitution of the
Articles of Confederation by strengthening the hand of the
central government and by limiting the powers of states, but it
did not incorporate some of Madison's stronger nationalistic
recommendations. Despite John Marshall, despite President
Jackson's strong stand against South Carolina's nullification

of a federal tariff, despite the Union's triumph in the Civil War over the ultimate encroachment (secession), despite the widespread nationalization of American life that we have seen in the twentieth century, petty encroachments are a continuing complaint. The relative success of the new Constitution in diminishing the worst kind of encroachment should not make one lose sight of the point that such intrusions would have been even more effectively stopped if Madison's stronger nationalistic recommendations of 1787 had been adopted.

By and large, the problem of violation of union treaties by the states is no longer a major problem. This is true even though, in Indian matters and in such historic instances as a Missouri violation of a United States-Canadian bird migration treaty, the nation has from time to time been plagued by this evil.

However, the vice of states trespassing upon each other's rights is another matter. The states are still guilty of this political vice, albeit to a lesser degree than in Madison's day. Madison saw in 1787 that a lack of harmony in economic matters was an inherent evil of a federal system, particularly when the conflict and competition of state laws militated against the common interest of the nation. States might not respect each other's laws in a whole host of matters—trade, taxation, navigation, slaves, free Negroes. Although the issue of slaves is no longer a legal and social problem, states today do not always respect each other's divorce laws or trucking laws, to take two glaring examples. And although the United States Constitution seeks to maximize respect for mutual state rights by insisting that "Full faith and credit shall be given in each State to the public Acts, Records, and judicial Proceedings of every other State," and by holding that the "Citizens of each State shall be entitled to all Privileges and Immunities of Citizens in the several States," this has by no means limited state trespasses on each other's rights.

Another vice, that of "want of common concert where the common interest requires it," calls attention to what is perhaps Madison's most perceptive point in his analysis of disunion. Here he called for sweeping national power in matters of common interest. Such power was essential to unite and advance the union. Madison saw this in 1787 and later in

71

the 1820s and 1830s. Without national power to provide "common concert" in matters of "common interest," the union would disintegrate. There would be different laws in different states on issues that called for a national, uniform policy. A nationalist court under Marshall would work hard to advance "common concert," but it alone would not be able to avert the catastrophe of civil war. The nationalization of American life on matters of common interest that reached a climax in the twentieth century confirms the accuracy of Madison's original position in 1787.

Undoubtedly, the new Constitution was an improvement in securing "common concert" in matters of "common interest." Yet it is clear that the nation stopped short of the broader nationalization called for by Madison's diagnosis in 1787. Here one encounters one of the ironies of American history, which has been interpreted as a melodrama with Madison in the role of villain. One critic has argued that this vice, along with most of the others in Madison's classic statement, would not be so troublesome today if Madison himself had not later warped the original broad meaning of Congressional power.

Madison's later changes of viewpoint on the question of national power did have the ultimate effect of limiting the ability of the central government to act where common interest required such action. In 1787 Madison saw the vice. What changed after 1787 was not Madison's diagnosis but political conditions which dictated a course of action different from that suggested by his strong nationalism of 1787. From the perspective of a thoughtful nationalist it is perhaps ironic— but not sinful—that some of Madison's best laid nationalist plans went awry, that he was rebuffed several times by a majority in the Convention, and that fears of the Federalist program required him to emphasize limited constitutional construction in the 1790s.

However, in Madison's defense several additional observations are relevant here. If Madison had been doctrinaire in the 1790s, he would not have budged from his strong nationalism of 1787. This might have left Congress with more power to cope with national problems. However, the more likely conjecture is *either* that Madison would have been pushed down the political drain by the real states' rights men *or* that America would have moved toward the "high-toned" government which Hamilton favored. Under these circumstances Congress might have achieved power at the expense of republicanism or might have been dangerously stripped of power. When these possibilities are noted and the amplitude of present congressional power is stressed, adverse criticism of Madison on this point loses a great deal of its force.

The nation has also made great strides in connection with "a guarantee to the States of their republican constitutions and laws against internal violence." Unhappily, even if state governments have been more stable since 1787, they have not uniformly exemplified reasonable majority rule. Too often Right and Power have not been combined. It is certainly a tribute to Madison's political genius that he noted that a republican union could not long remain either republican or united unless the states that composed it were both popular and stable.

The problem of a sanction in the laws and coercion in the government of the Union seems to be one that has been largely eliminated until one calls to mind the American Civil War or, in more modern times, the massive resistance to public school integration in the 1950s and 1960s. It should be noted here that the Civil War demonstrated dramatically— and tragically—the correctness of Madison's diagnosis. It was the very catastrophe Madison had sought to avoid. If the absurdity of unanimity had been recognized (and nullification and secession repudiated by all the states), the law of the Union honored, and the Union's use of force to uphold law respected, then a solution other than a bloody civil war might have been forthcoming. Southern resistance to integration after the 1954 Supreme Court decision on public school segregation illustrates the difficulties still facing the implementation of the principle of legal sanction and governmental coercion in the absence of social consensus and prudent leadership in support of the "due supremacy" of the nation. The events that confronted President Kennedy at Oxford, Mississippi, and President Eisenhower at Little Rock, Arkansas, and President Lincoln at Fort Sumter, South Carolina, show that Madison's recognition that a republican federal union will collapse unless it can invoke force to uphold the law of the nation is a permanent insight into the new federalism that emerged in 1787.

The problem of lack of popular ratification of the basic charter of government disappeared with the acceptance of the new constitution by the people through their representatives in the ratifying conventions in the thirteen states. The objective of such popular ratification, Madison clearly saw, was broad, national support for the supreme law of the land and a sense of national obligation to obey such law. Unless the new union was frankly based on such popular support, a truly republican union could not endure.

Finally, what can be said of the multiplicity, mutability, and injustice of the laws of the states? Too many laws, laws too changeable, unjust laws—these, Madison held, were the diseases of the body politic under the government of the Articles of Confederation. Although the virulence of these diseases today is not comparable to their malignancy before 1787, complaints still abound. The comments made earlier with regard to common interest, congressional power, and state encroachments apply here too. Madison saw the problem and proposed a remedy. His remedy was not fully adopted in 1787; nor has Congress always invoked the ample powers it now has to cope with the situation first noted in 1787. Yet the course of American history demonstrates increasingly greater national efforts to protect the basic rights of all Americans and to achieve a common policy where common national problems demand such a policy.

Madison's analysis of the underlying "treaty" theory of the old Confederation has, therefore, proved to be highly relevant. He revealed the state of disunion under the Articles of Confederation. He subsequently highlighted the disruption and breakup threatened by Calhoun and his followers. He clarified the weaknesses of any federal structure, any division of power between the center and the circumference; and he pointed to the principles and policies essential to curtail and overcome these weaknesses. His was not, and is not, a flawless solution to the federal problem. At best there are only proximate solutions to insoluble problems. Nonetheless, his understanding of the dangers of disunion provides continuing illumination of a republican and federal state because it was rooted in a political theory which came to grips with the central difficulties of attempting to reconcile liberty and empire in a large state.

Madison's failures in 1787 should not blind us to his federal perceptions, as his successes should not lead us to ignore the inevitable friction inherent in a federal system which divides power between a central government and its component states. Madison understood better than most the possible flaws in the evolving theory of federal union. In the absence of a national veto, he foresaw an inevitable struggle for power between nation and states which, unless checked, could lead to a decision by force of arms only. Thus, he insisted quite early that federal theory must make the nation the judge of the rules by which the federal game was to be played. Nullification, he urged later in life, was to be rejected precisely because it proposed that the nation not be this judge. Today a nationalistic Supreme Court, generally reflecting national public opinion, congressional ethos, and presidential power, functions to guard against the evils of disunion that Madison sought to avoid. This may obscure the fact that the Supreme Court's generally respected position as one crucial umpire of our federal system was assured by the Union's victory in the Civil War. Such a war Madison had hoped to avoid. The Court, we must not forget, was unable to prevent it. To note this is not to argue that Madison's "federal negative" would have been workable and effective in averting such a conflict. It is, however, to suggest the correctness of Madison's analysis of disunion and his recognition of the need for a device that would effectively prevent encroachment "of the States on the general authority, sacrifices of the national to local interests." The problem of umpiring the federal system persists. The problem of national-state harmony persists. The problem of due national supremacy persists. Madison's political heritage—in 1787 and in the 1830s—can inspire us to respond prudently to these problems, even if we appreciate that there is no permanent solution to the insoluble problems of politics in a federal state.

CHAPTER 4

The New Federalism

> *"The proposed Constitution, therefore, is, in strictness, neither a national nor a federal Constitution, but a composition of both."*
>
> — *The Federalist,* Number 39

I

In this chapter I should like first to concentrate on the actual operative principles of the new federal system that emerged from the deliberations of the Philadelphia Convention—the principles that were defended by Madison primarily in *The Federalist.* I should like to point out how Madison saw these principles operating to deal with the difficulty of republican government in a large country, and how these principles successfully divided power between a central government and its component states in a way that would be satisfactory to both. The new federalism, then, would not only be a response to disunion—as I have suggested in the preceding chapter—but also to large size. I shall single out for special attention the cardinal propositions that would guide the functioning of the new federalism: (1) the unique division of powers between nation and states; (2) the direct operation of federal law on the individuals of the union; (3) the amplitude and elasticity of national power; (4) the robust pragmatic temper that must guide judgment of the proper operation of the new federal system; (5) the experimental character of the new federal laboratory; (6) the Supreme Court's crucial role in maintaining the proper division of powers in the federal union; (7) the role of consensus in ensuring the new federalism's success.

Although my primary concern in the first portion of this chapter will be the new federalism of the Constitution of 1787 as explained by Madison in *The Federalist,* I will have occasion to note, particularly in the second part of this chapter, Madison's shift in interpretation: first in the 1790s and then, again, in the 1820s and 1830s. This shift occurs largely on the question of the amplitude and elasticity of national power and the proper mode of response to such power in a federal system.

Secondly, I should like to use Madison's shifts in constitutional interpretation, largely in the 1790s, to examine the criticism of Madison's position on the new federalism by two groups of critics. In the first group are those who condemn his retreat on the scope of national power in the 1790s. In the second group are those modern states' rights advocates who profess to see in that retreat a defense of their own severely limited interpretation of national power and their view of state power. My objective will be to use these two points of view to delineate more accurately the strengths and weaknesses of Madison's actual position.

In the next chapter, Chapter 5, I will set forth Madison's *empirical theory.* This theory explains why the new republican and federal government would, indeed, work to control faction which threatened union, a successful division of power between nation and states, and the maintenance of just and popular government. In Chapter 6 I will deal more fully with Madison's efforts to counter what he deemed the anti-republican danger to the new republic. Together these chapters present the fuller political theory of the man who was not only the Father of the Constitution but also several other fathers as well. He was also a Father of American Union, a Father of Modern Nationalism, a Father of Modern Federalism, and a Father of Republican Party Opposition.

II

In Number 39 *Federalist,* one finds the clearest delineation of the "middle-ground" solution to the problem of republican governments in a large federal state, which the Constitution actually embodied. Madison was now writing in support of a document which was probably more "federal" (or confederate) and less "national" (or centralized) than he had ideally preferred. He was, moreover, now seeking in *The Federalist* to answer those anti-Federalist opponents of the proposed new constitution who argued that it ought to "have preserved the *federal* form, which regards the Union as a *Confederacy* of sovereign states; instead of which they have framed a *national* government, which regards the Union as a *consolidation* of the States." [1]

Madison's argument in Number 39 *Federalist* demonstrated that the anti-Federalists were both right and wrong. They were right in believing that the new constitution possessed some radically new nationalistic features. They were wrong in holding that it would set up what amounted to a consolidated government.

What, then, was the unique division of powers between nation and states? In masterful fashion, Madison argued that the new constitution "is, in strictness, neither a national nor a federal Constitution, but a combination of both." [2] It is extremely important to note here that Madison was not necessarily stating the accepted meaning of these terms in 1787 and 1788, but rather the meaning they have acquired since he wrote the article. Before he wrote, these terms were fluid and ambiguous. *The Federalist* first gave them precision, and experience under the new constitution provided for them a more concrete reference. It is not an exaggeration to say that the meaning of the word "federalism" in the modern world can be traced to Madison's definition and explanation in *The Federalist*. [3]

"In its foundation," Madison pointed out, the Constitution "is federal" because the people as composing the states, "not as individuals composing one entire nation," ratified the Constitution. In the source of its power, the Constitution is "partly federal and partly national" for three reasons. First, the members of the House of Representatives were chosen by the people of the states. The number of representatives allotted each state was to be roughly in proportion to each state's population. Second, Senators (at this time) were to be chosen by state legislators. (This provision, of course, was subsequently changed by the Seventeenth Amendment, ratified in 1913, which enabled the people of the states to elect their Senators directly.) Third, the President was chosen by electors from the states, electoral votes being weighted both as to population and statehood. In the operation of its powers, the Constitution was national because its powers affected "individual citizens composing the nation, in their individual capacities." However, the Constitution was federal with regard to the extent of its powers because the jurisdiction of the central government "extends to certain enumerated objects only, and leaves to the several States a residuary and inviolable sovereignty over all other objects." Finally, amendments to the Constitution were neither wholly federal nor wholly national, for they could not be made by a "majority of the people of the Union" and did not require a "concurrence of each State in the Union," but instead required action by both the central government and the states.[4]

For skill of analysis, clarity of exposition, and brevity of discussion, Number 39 *Federalist* has no rival as a statement of the principles of American federal union. Here Madison formally illuminated the foundations of the new federal system, its source of power, pattern of operation, extent of powers, and manner of amendment. Here Madison defended a unique idea in political theory. Here, perhaps, is America's most seminal contribution to operational political science in the modern world. And although all the ideas that went into this classic formulation cannot be attributed to Madison alone, his preeminent role in that formulation is unmistakable.

The significance of a new central government able to operate directly on the individuals composing the states of the new federal union has been mentioned above and has been noted in the preceding chapter. Here it is important only to emphasize that this operational feature of the new federalism enabled the central government to reach the individual citizens of the union directly and immediately without the intervention of state governments. Money could be raised without having to rely upon state taxes and treasuries. And national law, affecting the individuals of the nation, would be obeyed throughout the union, honored by state officials, and directly enforced by national officers.

The direct operation of national law on the individuals composing the union becomes even more significant in consideration of Madison's view of the amplitude and elasticity of national power. Madison held that the new constitution provided for ample but limited powers, for generous yet enumerated powers. Here Madison toned down the strong nationalism of the Convention; yet he did not budge on the need for broad, national powers to cope with matters of national concern.

In *The Federalist,* Madison clearly conceded—again and again—that the new constitution provided for a central government of limited and enumerated powers; it did not abolish the governments of the separate states:

> ... The general government is not to be charged with the whole power of making and administrating laws. Its jurisdiction is limited to certain enumerated objects, which concern all the members of the republic, but which are not to be attained by the separate provisions of any. The subordinate governments, which can extend their care to all those other objects which can be separately provided for, will retain their due authority and activity. Were it proposed by the plan of the convention to abolish the governments of the particular States, its adversaries would have some ground for objection; though it would not be difficult to show that if they were abolished the general government would be compelled, by the principle of self-preservation, to reinstate them in their proper jurisdictions.[5]

Madison was particularly aware of the arduous "task of marking the proper line of partition between the authority of the general and that of the State governments." He had sought greater powers for the central government in the Convention; now, however, he was prepared to accept the compromise reached in Philadelphia. Madison was most certainly speaking for himself, as well as for others, when he concluded Number 37 *Federalist* with the observation "that all the deputations composing the convention were satisfactorily accommodated by the final act, or were induced to accede to it by a deep conviction of the necessity of sacrificing private opinions and partial interests to the public good, and by a despair of seeing this necessity diminished by delays or by new experiments." [6]

Nonetheless, Madison still took a very generous view of
the need for national power to advance the public good, and of
such key constitutional clauses as the "necessary and proper"
clause. And he did not hesitate to call a spade a spade. He
spoke out frankly against a foolish notion of state sovereignty.
He rebuked those who would not endorse elastic governmental
means to achieve legitimate national ends.

"Was, then, the American Revolution affected," he
wrote in Number 45 *Federalist,* "was the American Confederacy formed, was the precious blood of thousands spilt, and
the hard-earned substance of millions lavished, not that the
people of America should enjoy peace, liberty, and safety, but
that the government of the individual states, that particular
municipal establishments, might enjoy a certain extent of
power, and be arrayed with certain dignities and attributes of
sovereignty?" The "solid happiness of the people" was not to
be sacrificed on the thirteen altars of state sovereignty. The
public good was supreme, "and no form of government whatsoever has any other value than as it may be fitted for the
attainment of this object." Madison did not mince words.
". . . As far as the sovereignty of the States cannot be reconciled to the happiness of the people, the voice of every good
citizen must be, Let the former be sacrificed to the latter." If
Madison ever repudiated this public statement in Number 45
Federalist, I am not aware of it.[7]

In a similar vein, Madison recognized the need for positive substantive powers in the new central government to
enable it to triumph over the state of disunion and to meet the
changing needs of the nation. In writing about the "necessary
and proper" clause—the clause which states that Congress
shall have power "To make all laws which shall be necessary
and proper for carrying into execution" the national government's enumerated powers—Madison held that "Without the
substance of this power, the whole Constitution would be a
dead letter." A constitution must be "accommodated . . . not
only to the existing state of things, but to all the possible
changes that futurity may produce. . . ." "No axiom is more
clearly established in law, or in reason, than that wherever the
end is required, the means are authorized: wherever a general
power to do a thing is given, every particular power necessary

for doing so is included." [8] Thus Madison laid down the axiom of interpretation which Hamilton and Marshall were subsequently to employ in a strong nationalist defense of such Federalist party measures as the national bank.

Madison in *The Federalist* was a moderate nationalist who wanted generous and elastic national powers to advance the broad ends of the national union. At this time he was not greatly worried about the abuse of these powers because the prime evils that worried him arose in the states. Nonetheless, it is interesting to note, in the paragraph of Number 44 *Federalist* quoted above, that his broad interpretation of the necessary and proper clause raised the possibility of the misconstruction of this power. Was this simply the politician's sensitivity to the effect of his nationalistic interpretation upon his states' rights readers? Or had Madison, the scholarly political theorist, already looked ahead to anticipate trouble in an unwarranted expansion of national power for anti-republican ends? Perhaps both political sensitivity and theoretical prophecy were involved here. Perhaps both were involved because Madison remained the prudent politician who knew that republican politics must meet with the approval of a republican electorate and be based upon republican principles of protest. If the federal government should misconstrue and thus overstep its legitimate powers, he wrote, the state legislatures "will be ever ready to mark the innovation, to sound the alarm to the people, and to exert their local influence in effecting a change of federal representatives." Here, already, in the classic account of federalism, was one of the germs of the Virginia Resolutions. [9]

Madison's approach to the new federalism was pragmatic. The powers of the central government and of the state governments would, in the last analysis, depend upon their success in doing a job for their respective constituents. Here, then, dogmatic views on the sovereignty of the states, or on the powers of the central government, must give way to the political realities which suggest the means to be employed in advancing the needs and aspirations of people for peace, liberty, and prosperity. In the natural, pragmatic competition between the central and state governments for the advancement of the happiness of the people, the states need not fear that their powers would be destroyed. They had many natural advantages in such healthy competition. State governments were closer to the people. State leaders knew the people better. State officials had more rewards to offer and more services to render. All that they had to do was a good job in the eyes of their constituents. "If, therefore ... the people should in the future become more partial to the federal government than to the State governments, the change can only result from such manifest and irresistible proofs of a better administration, as will overcome all their antecedent propensities. And in that case, the people ought not surely to be precluded from giving most of their confidence where they may discover it to be most due." [10]

This same pragmatic temper would also suffuse the experimental character of the new federal system. The varying governments in the new union constituted so many unique governmental laboratories, wherein successful experiments in one government might be copied by others, and wherein dangerous experiments would be limited and contained by the insulation provided by multiple governments. As Madison put the point in later life, the federal system encouraged "local experiments" which, "if failing, are but a partial and temporary evil; if successful, may become a common and lasting improvement." The federal system, he wrote, "excites emulation without enmity." It provided opportunities to try out various ideas—some good, some bad—as they flowed from a heterogeneous people. Happily, the dangerous practices in a given state could inflict only limited harm. If popular insurrections broke out in one state, he wrote in Number 43 *Federalist*, they could be quelled by other states. Similarly, abuses in part of the nation could be reformed by the remaining sounder parts. This notion of federalism as a governmental laboratory, wherein a diverse, republican people may experiment in the ways of free government, was very congenial to Madison. Throughout his life he played variations on this theme. [11]

Within limits, the states were free to experiment within a federal system. The system would operate to encourage sound, and discourage unsound, experiments. Another feature of the system that would operate to keep the states in their proper places, and to arbitrate clashes between the nation and the states, was the Supreme Court. "Some such tribunal is clearly essential," Madison wrote in Number 39 *Federalist,* "to prevent an appeal to the sword and a dissolution of the compact. . . ." This meant, in effect, that the Court would function as an organ that operated to keep the states in their respective places. It would serve as an arbiter of the federal system. If Madison was occasionally unhappy about some of the Court's decisions, by the 1830s—especially with respect to the talk about nullification—he clearly supported the need to give to the "Judicial authority of the U.S." the power "to provide for a peaceful and authoritative termination" of "controversies concerning the boundary of Jurisdiction" between nation and states. "A uniform authority of the laws," he maintained, "is in itself a vital principle." Without it, some "of the most important laws could not be . . . executed." They must, he insisted, "be executed in all the States or they could be duly executed in none." The federal courts alone could not successfully hold the nation together, but, in conjunction with other organs and ideas, they had a vital role to play in maintaining the new federal union of states. The courts represented a feasible alternative to anarchy in deciding jurisdictional disputes. The courts offered a feasible way to avoid a disastrous diversity on fundamental matters of national policy. They provided a practical solution to inconvenient, expensive, constitutional amendment. They suggested a reasonable technique for avoiding a return to the "treaty" concept, which required negotiation between the Union and the states.[12]

However, if the federal courts could help to umpire the federal system, they would be successful, Madison recognized, only if there was an underlying consensus in the new nation on key matters. Such consensus constituted the broad base of popular support which made a republican government responsive, strong, and effective. It is indeed unfortunate that Madison's rhetorical appeals for this consensus should often be interpreted as deceitful propaganda rather than as an artful combination of honest conviction and prudent communication. Madison consciously recognized as part of his new federal theory the importance of agreement on certain fundamentals. These fundamentals held the Union together. Such consensus was a major prerequisite for the success of the new federal and republican constitution. Without shared emotions, mutual trust and regard, agreed principles, the Union would disintegrate. It would lack the shared confidence and convictions that enable differing peoples in different states and with different interests to operate the new system.

One of the most important fundamentals was a sense of American nationality. In Number 14 *Federalist,* Madison had stressed the "many chords of affection" that "knit together" the people of America. He had called to mind the "kindred blood which flows in the veins of American citizens, the mingled blood which they have shed in defense of their sacred rights, [and which] consecrate[s] their Union." In Number 43 *Federalist,* he had argued that "considerations of a common interest, and above all, the remembrance of endearing scenes which are past" would help to triumph over the "obstacles to reunion" between the ratifying states and those that might not initially become parties to the new Union. The sacred rights of which Madison spoke were republican rights. They were American rights. They were rights inherent in a republican system upon which all Americans were in general agreement. American nationality, and all that this might mean for internal peace and external respect, for domestic justice and general prosperity, would be an emotional as well as a rational tie holding the new federal nation together. Here, then, emotionally supercharged with an American patriotism, was the agreement on enough fundamentals essential to the new republic. Some interests might divide a large and diverse nation, but essential interests united the nation. Differences and dissensions were to be expected. But enough kindred interests—political, economic, social, and religious, common to all parts of the Union—remained to knit the nation together, and to make republican government in a large state possible.[13]

III

The consensus that Madison saw as essential for the operation of the new federalism has not characterized Madison's critics. He has sometimes been attacked as a villain by strong nationalists and occasionally invoked as a demi-hero by advocates of states' rights. By and large, their reaction to Madison's statement of the new federalism is not based on the federalism he defended in *The Federalist*—the "middle-ground" course that the Convention took in 1787—but upon his interpretations in the 1790s, when he turned against the Federalist party policies of Hamilton and his extremist Federalist allies. Strong nationalists today see in Madison's shift a desertion of his own strong nationalism which he brought to the Philadelphia Convention. Modern advocates of states' rights see in Madison's endorsement of strict constitutional construction, state protest, and interposition a defense of their own views of federal union. These two polar positions provide one with an opportunity to examine Madison's changing views on the new federalism—first in the 1790s and later in his life—and thus to assess the strengths and weaknesses of his fuller views of a federal system as a response to the problem of reconciling liberty and large size.

Modern critics in the strongly nationalist school of constitutional interpretation, e.g., W. W. Crosskey, in his *Politics and the Constitution,* would have us believe that the enumeration and division of powers, as classically understood, did not significantly restrict a strongly nationalist central government. This interpretation is based upon the alleged contemporary meaning of key words like "commerce" and a presumed plot by Madison to warp the broad meaning of the original constitutional document. They have seen in Madison's subsequent interpretation of the "necessary and proper" and "general welfare" clauses, at the time of his battle against the Hamiltonian program and the Alien and Sedition Acts, a rejection of his earlier and wiser nationalism. This apostasy, they contend, was largely responsible for the subsequent inability of the national government to meet national problems. Had Madison stuck to his earlier nationalist interpretation all would have been well for the development of a union in which the national government would have been equipped to cope with national problems. However, so their argument runs, this was not to be the case. Instead, Madison adopted a restricted interpretation of federal power and this had the effect of retarding the development of that more nearly perfect union which Madison himself had earlier advocated.[14]

Critics in the states' rights school, on the other side of the political fence, have stressed Madison's strict constitutional interpretation of the 1790s, have relished his use of state protests against tyrannical national legislation, and have resuscitated his ambiguous doctrine of interposition, all in an effort to buttress their arguments against national civil rights actions and (what they deem) other obnoxious federal legislation. This strategy is only a more modern application of the states' rights doctrine which has generally been employed to delay, frustrate, and defeat measures of the central government which threaten vested interests in the states. Consequently, those in this school play up the alleged states' rights aspects of Madison's concept of federal union, and ignore Madison's own earlier nationalism; just as the strong nationalists emphasize that earlier nationalism and condemn Madison for his subsequent backsliding. By and large, the strong nationalists tend to be liberal or radical in their political orientation, the states' rights people conservative or reactionary.[15]

Both interpretations of Madison—and the significance of his shift in the 1790s—are misleading. Both lead to a distorted picture of Madison's "middle-ground" conception of the more nearly perfect union. Both ignore or incompletely interpret the historical scene which conditioned the evolution of Madison's political theory.

There can be little doubt that Madison's lifelong commitment to due national supremacy predisposed him to accept a nationalistic interpretation of the Constitution. However, as I have already pointed out on the basis of his position in *The Federalist*, this did not mean that the states were to be obliterated or to be transformed into nullities or administrative puppets of the central government on all key matters. Certainly this was not Madison's position at the time he wrote his numbers for *The Federalist*, which was to become for him an authoritative interpretation of the new federal system. The states, then, were not to be liquidated as "sovereign" powers (within their sphere of legitimate authority) or to be reduced to mere administrative arms of an all-powerful central government. These strongly nationalist critics ignore the fact that the federal union that Madison finally came to defend in Number 39 *Federalist* was a "partly federal and partly national" remedy, that the "proposed Constitution . . . is, in strictness, neither a national nor a federal Constitution, but a composition of both." [16]

On the other side, there can be little doubt that Madison endorsed strict constitutional construction in his partisan battles against most of the Hamiltonian program and against the Alien and Sedition Acts; that he did encourage the people of the states to repudiate these measures; and that he did advocate interposition against federal tyranny in the case of the Alien and Sedition Acts. But this by no means justified nullification and secession in Madison's eyes; and, to extrapolate, it would not—in connection with the integration controversy—sanction opposition to the due supremacy of the Union as interpreted by the Supreme Court. These conclusions become more convincing, I believe, if one calls to mind the events that led to Madison's reaction to the Hamiltonian program and to the Alien and Sedition Acts, measures which were quite different in character from the Supreme Court's desegregation decisions or national legislation on civil rights. Madison was defending civil liberties, not trying to oppose protection of basic human rights; he was attacking, not defending, vested-interest legislation. These conclusions are also supported by examining more critically—and much more carefully—what Madison actually said both in the 1790s and later in his life.

What the "high-toned" nationalists today fail fully to comprehend is that points of view that might be maintained with perfect consistency in the certain world of theory must often be modified, pursuant to excellent logic, in the contingent world of practice. Politics, in and after the Convention, did indeed lead Madison to modify his own strong nationalism and to give a more confederate substance to his still-fluid federal theory. He did this in order to win with an imperfect constitution rather than to fail with an ideal one. He understood that only a more moderate nationalistic interpretation would meet with success. The shift here was no unholy plot, but simple political foresight. Similarly, politics in the 1790s suggested to him a yet more confined view of national power than he had enunciated in *The Federalist*. Here, again, there was no diabolical plot but a response to the dynamic forces of American politics. This response seemed prudent to Madison in the 1790s, although we may have our doubts on this point as Monday morning quarterbacks enjoying a retrospective view of American history.

An illustration of my argument is Madison's interpretation in the 1790s of the "necessary and proper" and "general welfare" clauses in the historical context of Hamilton's efforts to implement his stake-in-society theory. This theory was based upon the premise that statesmanship consisted in rallying to the cause of a strong, respected, and prosperous nation those wealthy, active, interested groups which would benefit financially from national policies as the nation benefited. Madison clearly sought to limit Hamilton's nationalistic interpretation of these clauses, at this time, because he feared Hamilton's alleged anti-republican program, not a nationalistic interpretation for proper republican ends. Perhaps Madison erred in interpreting these clauses as he did in the 1790s. This interpretation did contrast with his own more nationalistic outlook, including his viewpoint in *The Federalist*. Yet in the context of the political fight against the Hamiltonian Federalists, when both sides naturally sought all available weapons, Madison could quite understandably foresee an evil in the broadly nationalistic use of these clauses for allegedly plutocratic and even tyrannical ends. Before critics berate Madison too hard for his limited vision in the early 1790s, they should remember that he also used strict construction against the Alien and Sedition Acts, acts which few strong nationalists are willing to defend today.

On second glance, it might seem that Madison's arguments on behalf of strict constitutional interpretation are not quite as unreasonable as the strong nationalists make them out to be. Indeed, in general and divorced from such particular measures as the first bank bill, which Madison—perhaps unwisely—opposed, much in his arguments might still be accepted by a nationalist who is not a "consolidationist." Thus, Madison's general constitutional posture was unassailable. He wanted to maintain a government of limited powers.

Hence, he accepted as indispensable the "necessary and proper" clause but opposed any construction of it that would give to Congress an "unlimited discretion." So far, so good. Then, however, Madison proceeded to define necessary and proper in too limited a fashion. Implied powers must naturally, obviously, appropriately, directly, evidently, and immediately pertain to the Constitution's delegated powers. The tie between the delegated powers and the implied powers must be obvious if the government were to remain one of enumerated, limited powers. Implied powers that were merely convenient or conducive to the exercise of delegated powers were not necessary and proper. The "necessary and proper" clause should not be used to support a "distinct," "independent," "substantive," "great and important" power in contrast to an "accessory or subaltern" power.[17]

So understood, this interpretation is, therefore, at odds with even the more moderate nationalism that Madison defended in *The Federalist.* It is a crabbed interpretation of the Constitution. It is not in the spirit of Madison's own early nationalism which Hamilton advocated so brilliantly and which Marshall wrote into the guiding decisions of the Supreme Court in *McCulloch* v. *Maryland* (1819). Superficially, Madison's interpretation is most reasonable when it is divorced from such specific measures as the bank bill, which it was voiced to oppose—a national bank which Madison, ironically, had himself advocated earlier. However, as an interpretation which has the practical effort—in the hands of strict constructionists—of limiting the power of the national government to cope with national problems, it merits the adverse criticisms which the strong nationalists, from Marshall to the present, have consistently leveled against it.

In connection with the "general welfare" clause, Madison held that there was no blanket power to spend for measures related to the general welfare, but only a power to spend for the general welfare as the general welfare was explained and limited by the specifically enumerated powers of the Constitution. To Madison it made little difference whether the "general welfare" clause authorized every measure directly, or whether it merely authorized every measure for which money could be expended. Both interpretations

91

would transform a limited government into an unlimited government.[18]

Here, too, Madison's position of the 1790s has not been vindicated by our constitutional history. As Chief Justice Marshall accepted Hamilton's more generous view of the "necessary and proper" clause in *McCulloch* v. *Maryland* (1819), so the Supreme Court, speaking through Justice Roberts, in *United States* v. *Butler* (1936) endorsed Hamilton's more generous view of the spending power.

It is, of course, true that the effect of Madison's interpretation of these key clauses would have been to tie the hands of the national government. And in the early 1790s Madison did want to tie Hamilton's hands, as he sought from 1798 to 1800 to oppose the Alien and Sedition Acts. Alas, what Madison did not clearly appreciate was that this interpretation might also tie the hands of good, sound republicans when they sought to use the powers of the national government for good, sound republican ends. This point may also enable us to see that the later alleged backsliding of Jefferson and Madison, when they came to power, may be interpreted in a more favorable light. Instead of the infidelity which John Randolph saw, there was simply a somewhat embarrassing recognition that there was nothing wrong with a broader exercise of national power for rightful republican ends. Indeed, such a recognition is a constant theme in the history of American party politics when the "outs" come to power. Nonetheless, it is true that strict construction did become a feature of the Republican party of Jefferson and Madison and did hold up national support of many projects—e.g., a national system of roads and canals—which most observers today would agree were in the national interest.

With hindsight it is easy for modern nationalist critics to say: Madison was wrong. The very "due supremacy" of the nation, for which he fought in 1787, could not be maintained unless the Constitution were interpreted more liberally than he suggested in the 1790s. Without such a broader and more liberal interpretation the nation would not be able to cope with national needs, and the states would not have the constitutional authority or financial resources to attend to pressing matters of nationwide concern, to achieve salutary uniform standards, or to resist anti-republican tendencies. Congress needs broad discretion in spending for the general welfare. Congress needs broad discretion in passing laws "necessary and proper" to carry out its delegated powers, Hence, instead of indiscriminately attacking the constitutionality of both the Hamiltonian program and the Alien and Sedition Acts, Madison should have been more selective. He should have attacked only the *wisdom* of specific measures that were part of the Hamiltonian program. He should have restricted his constitutional attack to the Sedition Act, the most vulnerable of all Federalist measures. For is it not clear that his constitutional attack against the Hamiltonian program contradicted his own nationalistic insights, even though it supported his political attack against what he thought was an unwise and fundamentally anti-republican program?

If Madison had restricted his constitutional attack to the arena of civil liberties and his attack on the wisdom of Hamiltonian measures to the arena of economic, political, and social policy, then all would have been well. Then, when the Republicans came to power they would have been unembarrassed about a liberal interpretation of key constitutional clauses in the field of economic, political, and social policy. Madison would then have been free as President to sign, instead of to veto, an internal improvements bill (the Bonus Bill of 1817), which he recognized was essential to the cohesiveness of the nation. He recognized this bill as wise and necessary for the growth and prosperity of the West and the nation, but felt compelled to veto it on constitutional grounds—because of the lack of more explicit constitutional power to spend money for roads and canals. Politics did thus in the 1790s create for Madison a Procrustean bed of constitutional interpretation which was to torture him in later life.

Certain reflections will, however, enable one to understand Madison's position, even if one disagrees with his commitment in the 1790s to a more narrow interpretation of national power. In 1787 his concern for power in the possession of the central government was dictated by a desire to strengthen and preserve a union that would not succumb to dissolution, a union that would work out an equitable balance between necessary power in a central government and autonomy for the states in matters of local concern. This was the central objective in 1787. This objective was designed to reconcile the power essential to govern a large nation with the liberty that must be left to people to conduct their own, more local affairs. Increased power for the central government was an indispensable means to accomplish this objective in 1787. By the 1790s, however, largely as a result of the adoption of the Constitution, the central government had been considerably strengthened. Hence, the overriding need for power was no longer present. Indeed, in the 1790s, Madison felt that the central government was going too far. Now it was not strengthening the federal union by the exercise of legitimate powers but undermining a republican union by pursuing an anti-republican policy. Hence action must be taken to check such national power in the wrong hands.

Finally, it is important to note that Madison has not been entirely out of harmony with American history in his interpretation in the 1790s of those key clauses of the Constitution so meaningfully related to federalism. It is true that the nation has followed Hamilton's interpretation, but it has, particularly in modern times, utilized this interpretation to advance democratic ideas more in harmony with Madison's political philosophy. What is more, these clauses, broadly as they have been construed, have not been used to give Congress unlimited discretion—the arguments of current conservatives or reactionaries to the contrary! Bills based on the "necessary and proper" clause must still logically pertain to the Constitution's delegated powers, despite the fact that Congress' discretion in establishing pertinence is very broad indeed. Similarly, spending for the general welfare is usually informed by, if not restricted to, the enumerated powers of the Constitution, even though Congress' discretion here has been broader than its latitudinarian interpretation of the commerce clause. The nation has moved toward the position of Madison's own strong nationalism prior to the Philadelphia Convention, but it has not rejected the "middle-ground" partly federal, partly national system which Madison defended in *The Federalist,* even though it has for the most part repudiated Madison's strict constitutional interpretation of the 1790s. It has never accepted the high-toned "national" form which Hamilton favored in his one great speech in the Convention.[19] It has clearly turned its back on the Confederate form which the anti-Federalists supported. The principle of due national supremacy has in fact operated to increase greatly the powers of the central government. This has come, however, in response to the changing facts of our national life. They are comparable to those changing facts between 1781 and 1787 which first induced Madison to cast about for new principles which he might employ to shape the more nearly perfect union, one capable of preserving liberty and local autonomy in a national state strong enough to govern a large nation of diverse interests.

Can the modern advocates of states' rights correctly base their case either on the spirit or the letter of Madison's evolving views on the new federalism? As I have indicated above, a case for strict constitutional interpretation can be found in Madison's position in the 1790s, but this is not the position that supports the Southern attack on the tariff, or South Carolina's protest against the so-called "Tariff of Abominations." Madison never backtracked on his nationalistic views on the tariff or commerce power. Congress could indeed levy a tariff, although any particular tariff might be unwise.

As for interposition, Madison in his later life *explicitly* repudiated nullification. He held that the Constitution, a compact (but not a treaty!) made by the sovereign people of the states, created a union that did not permit a single state, as a matter of constitutional right, to nullify an act of the central government or to withdraw from the Union. Although sovereign power was divided by this compact between the central government and the states, the law of the central government, within its sphere of authority, was the supreme law of the land and must be obeyed until constitutionally overcome. In cases of controversy over respective state and national spheres of authority, he clearly stated in the 1830s, the Supreme Court provided for peaceful, authoritative, impartial, and effective arbitrament. A resort beyond the Supreme Court was constitutional amendment. An ultimate— and still somewhat mysterious—resort was the *collective* action of the sovereign people of the sovereign states who had made the original constitutional compact and who could explain and remake it as they saw fit. This was ultraconstitutional interposition. But the constitutional technique, Madison insisted, must "provide for a peaceful and authoritative termination" of controversies and must preserve uniformity of law and that unity and strength so essential to the more nearly perfect union.[20]

Madison's position was emphatic. Nullification and secession rested upon an historically inaccurate theory of indivisible sovereignty in the separate states. Nullification, as I have already noted in the preceding chapter, would have the effect of "putting powder under the Constitution and Union, and a match in the hand of every party to blow them up at pleasure." [21] Clearly, any kind of interposition that militated against uniformity of legitimate national law, that destroyed necessary national unity, and that corroded national strength was not sanctioned by Madison's Virginia Resolutions of 1798. Argument may, of course, rage over the meaning of "legitimate" but one point is obvious. Transparent attempts by *individual* states to evade a uniform ruling announced by an organ of the central government could only have the ultimate effect of establishing anew that principle of state sovereignty under which the government of the Articles of Confederation had floundered. The more nearly perfect union could be maintained only if there was concert, not lack of concert, in matters where the common interest required it. Except under rare circumstances, to be noted below, the law of the central government must be obeyed, not disobeyed or set aside. This conclusion follows from both the letter and the spirit of Madison's political theory.

National concert and obedience to law, Madison held, must prevail when a state remains within the Union and operates under the Union's constitution. Only the violation by the central government of such basic rights as freedom of speech, press, and communication permits an aggrieved party, after other orthodox constitutional techniques have been employed, to use—penultimately—ultraconstitutional interposition. Ultimately, of course, people in the states could invoke the *moral* right to revolt. Under conditions of substantial and unrelieved tyranny, then, those aggrieved might ultimately exercise their undeniable moral or natural right of revolution. Wisely, the aggrieved would not revolt unless they were a majority. Both interposition and revolution, however, must have as their objective the restoration of basic republican rights and uniform republican rule. Such interposition did not justify a *single state* in defying the will of the central government as expressed through the central government's authoritative and legitimate organs.[22]

Thus there is no support for the extreme states' rights position in Madison's evolving views on the new federalism. Moderately strict construction—yes! Nullification—no! Protest—yes! Single-state interposition—no! The moral or natural right to revolt—yes! The constitutional right to secede—no! Strong action to protect First-Amendment rights—yes!

If Madison's views on interposition provide no sanction for those Southern advocates of states' rights in the 1950s who attempted to use the term to give a pedigree of legitimacy to their resistance to national decisions—whether by Congress, President, or Supreme Court—relating to civil rights actions, so his program for accommodation of nation and states, center and circumference, North and South, indicates how far away he was from the diehard spirit of those modern Southern interpositionists. The problem of balancing local autonomy and national rule, sectional mores and uniform protection, individual freedom and centralized power—this was a key problem of the new federalism, and it called for prudent statesmanship. There would always be quarrels about the exact division of federal power, about its amplitude and elasticity, about which level of government can best do a given job, about the character of federal experiments, about the Supreme Court's role as umpire of the federal system, and about how to maintain that consensus essential for the continuing operation of a federal system. And this is why the spirit of accommodation that prudent statesmen bring to a sensitive yet crucial issue is so vitally important.

Madison envisaged the creation of sound public opinion, equitable and farsighted economic adjustment, and reliance upon various bonds of union. He urged the South not to exaggerate its sufferings, to understand the true causes of its distress, and to recoil before the dread consequences of dis-

97

union. He urged the North to adopt a spirit of moderation and to permit mutual concessions. Without ignoring the legitimate needs of American industry, defense, development, and foreign policy, he favored a reduction of the tariff. He suggested an equitable sharing of necessary economic burdens. He advocated a policy of economic accommodation which would draw the North and the South together in the bond of common economic interest. He even anticipated the South's shift to manufacturing. This change would serve to eliminate permanent discord based upon what some maintained was a permanent incompatibility of economic interests between an agrarian South and an industrial North. Although keenly aware of divisive forces, Madison recognized and relied upon geographical, economic, and social bonds as effective countervailing factors. He felt, for example, that the existence of religious denominations, located in various sections of the country, and a common sense of patriotism would help bind the nation's wounds and thus perpetuate the more nearly perfect federal union.[23]

IV

There can be little doubt that Madison's approach to the problem of free, popular government in a large and strong republican state represented a major breakthrough in the history of federal theory. The Constitution was a tremendous advance over the union of the Articles of Confederation. One can say this without deprecating the achievement of the Articles or accepting, uncritically, the picture of the horrors of life in the United States between 1781 and 1787. The key question is not really the well-being of the American nation prior to the Constitution of 1787, but the value of the Constitution for the future development of a strong and united country. Much to the initial regret of Madison himself in 1787, and of ardent nationalists subsequently, and perhaps because the anti-Federalists did not share the nationalist view of a greater centralization of power, the new federal union was more federal and less national than Madison had hoped. Yet it did constitute a significant advance. And it did embody a number of Madison's central, nationalistic insights. Politics did lead to changes in Madison's evolving notion of federal union. These changes can be traced through the Philadelphia Convention, *The Federalist,* the Virginia Ratifying Convention, the Federalist-Republican battle of the 1790s, the period of republican ascendency after 1800, and the prodromal signs of civil war in the 1820s and 1830s. Theory, after all, is not divorced from reality. It shapes and is shaped by political experience. It is ironic that Madison who has frequently been accused of being a narrow-minded constitutional pedant is also berated for his shifts on constitutional questions. Both his concern for the Constitution and his shifts were designed to maintain the more nearly perfect union.

With one major exception—i.e., the American Civil War—that new federal union has worked reasonably well. It is impossible to say now what would have happened if Madison's initial nationalism had prevailed in 1787. One hypothesis is that there would have been no new constitution if Madison's brand of strong nationalism had carried the day at the Convention. If such nationalism had triumphed in Philadelphia in 1787, an even more limited interpretation of national power than Madison's in the 1790s might have become dominant when the opponents of such nationalism came to office. And, if this had not happened, it is a likely conjecture that civil war might have broken out earlier. These are the fascinating and fruitful "ifs" of history which, in retrospect, illuminate its course by challenging one to consider hypothetical alternatives. It is much less hypothetical to argue that the Civil War came in spite of, not because of, Madison's theory of federal union. There is no legitimate line of intellectual descent between Madison and Calhoun.

To stimulate the historical imagination even more, one might also argue, perversely, that the heritage of limited national power can with equal justice be placed on the shoulders of Alexander Hamilton and the Federalist party! For it was Hamilton and the members of this party who provoked the political reaction that led to the Virginia Resolutions. Admittedly, this is a dangerous argument but, nonetheless, it highlights a kernel of truth. A job poorly done, from Madison's republican point of view, first created the distrust of national power which subsequently passed over into our

American heritage. And this distrust lingered on even after the republican ascendency was achieved as a result of Jefferson's presidential victory in 1800, and it was not routed until the nationalistic tendencies of modern life in the nineteenth and twentieth centuries again called for a wise and broad exercise of national power to cope with national problems.

At present, of course, Congress has ample power to cope with national problems. What it lacks, if anything, is the will and the wisdom to act. Federalism, nonetheless, has been and will remain a brake upon the more thorough nationalization of American life. It is, however, a brake that may be released or tightened under our federal Constitution. The fault (and the lack of a more thorough nationalization of certain key issues is a fault in some respects) is not in the federal system but in the political actors who operate under the federal Constitution. Politics, not the Constitution, is to blame! But who would have it otherwise in a democratic political community? The true task facing scholar and statesman alike is not to rediscover the original, hidden meaning of the Constitution of 1787—and the alleged villains who have obscured its strongly nationalistic powers—but to raise the sights of the nation—leaders and followers alike—to its true interests today.

These considerations indicate that there is a debit as well as a credit side to the new federalism. The Compromise of 1787 still gives the states an enormous power to frustrate the happiness of a numerical majority of the nation. Moreover, the federal system permits annoying inequalities in the fields of education, health, employment, housing, and recreation, for example. It militates against a more uniform protection of civil rights. It perpetuates petty despotisms which rightly seem momentous to those adversely affected. It gives disproportionate power to the rural states of the nation. And up until the Supreme Court's one man-one vote decision in *Reynolds* v. *Simms* (1964) it gave disproportionate power to the rural, and largely agricultural, inhabitants and interests within all states. And this is just a brief sampling of the defects of a federal system today. This is no light price to pay for a theory which attempts to strike a balance between center and circumference. Yet it is not clear that a unitary system—

our modern phrase for what Madison would have called a consolidated government—is free from defects. Federalism—for better or worse—seems to be a response to large size. And if the new federalism of 1787 had not been adopted then, we would probably have been forced to invent it subsequently.

When all is said and done, however, Madison's "middle-ground" approach to the problem of reconciling republicanism and large size still stands out as an historical contribution to federal theory of the first magnitude. His leap into the political dark in 1787 was a bold and essentially successful venture. He may have shifted from his early nationalism in the 1790s, but it is eternally to his credit that he returned to a more nationalistic conclusion in the last years of his life. It is for Americans in the twentieth century to note but not to carp at his misjudgments; to praise judiciously but not to worship blindly his achievements. It is for all Americans to catch again the spirit of creative political theory so well expressed in the last paragraph of number 14 *Federalist,* as Madison himself looked back on the experimental work of the Revolutionary Fathers. This was the voice of a great patriot who knew well that the new federal union was not immortal, that if Americans had been born free in a blessed land it would take faith and will and intelligence to improve and perpetuate that inheritance.

> Happily for America, happily, we trust, for the whole human race, they pursued a new and more noble course. They accomplished a revolution which has no parallels in the annals of human society. They reared the fabrics of governments which have no model on the face of the globe. They formed the design of a great Confederacy, which it is incumbent on their successors to improve and perpetuate. If their works betray imperfections, we wonder at the fewness of them. If they erred most in the structure of the Union, this was the work most difficult to be executed; this is the work, which has been new modelled by the act of your convention, and it is that act on which you are now to deliberate and to decide.[24]

CHAPTER 5

Faction and the
Extensive Republic

"In the extended republic of the United States, and among the great variety of interests, parties, and sects which it embraces, a coalition of a majority of the whole society could seldom take place on any other principles than those of justice and the general good. . . ."

— *The Federalist,* Number 51

I

Faction was a third major difficulty plaguing the attempt to reconcile liberty and authority in a large state. The mischievous operation of faction in the states was a fertile cause of disunion under the Articles of Confederation and then, later, during the controversy over nullification in the 1820s and the 1830s. Madison's reaction against faction in the states led him to endorse a policy of strong nationalism in 1787. This strong nationalism, as modified in the Philadelphia convention, became the new federalism of the Constitution of 1787. Madison's new federalism constituted in large part the *operational* principles of the new union. They embodied his plea for due national supremacy, and included a proper division of powers between nation and states, a government operating directly upon the people of the union, expanded national powers, a Supreme Court functioning as an arbiter of the federal system, a pragmatic and experimental approach to the performance of governmental tasks, and the need of underlying consensus. This is the way the new federalism would work. However, these principles of Madison's theory did not clearly and fully explain *why* the new system would function to control faction. It is to this question that we must now turn. In speaking to this question, Madison developed the largely *explanatory* aspect of his theory of the extensive republic.

The rest of this chapter will be devoted to Madison's republican diagnosis of faction, followed by his remedy for faction and an appraisal of that remedy.

II

The continuing problems that Madison faced in responding to the difficulty posed by faction can be best expressed in two classic conundrums: How can one obtain a just and stable government in a republican community? How can one reconcile republican rule with large size? Madison had the creative political genius to recognize the linkage between these problems and to formulate them as a single question. Can an extensive republic (republican rule in a country of large size) guard against the evils of faction (and thus advance just and stable republican rule)? Madison's answer was affirmative. He thus premised his explanatory theory—in answer to the leading question above—on the empirical relationship between the clash of contending interests in a large country and the neutralization of faction. In so doing, he became the first American (and perhaps the first ancient or modern) theorist of pluralism in the history of political theory.

In analyzing faction, Madison put to good use a number of insights which he had derived from his wide reading. He concurred with the classic conclusion that an agricultural society (with widespread ownership of property) was most conducive to just and stable republican government. He benefited from the classic recognition of the value for freedom of a balance of social classes. He made use of Aristotle's distinction between what one might call a representative republic and a direct democracy, and of Aristotle's dictum that no man is a fair judge in his own cause. He appreciated the worth of Hume's suggestion about indirect elections, the importance of many electoral districts, and the filter-like function of representation. He combined these insights with some other notions—a new federal division of power, augmented constitutional power, specific constitutional prohibitions, popular virtue, and separation of powers—to give empirical substance and compelling logic to Montesquieu's hint of the possibilities of an extensive republic and Hume's suggestion for dealing with factional evils. What is most intriguing here is how he selected the proper threads of previous political thought, combined them with American threads of experience, and wove them into a consistent theory which served to explain the workability of the new American constitution of 1787.

Madison's pluralism—and his empirical theory—owed a great debt to his religious convictions. The value of a multiplicity of religious sects for the preservation of religious liberty was a theme Madison grasped early, enunciated vigorously in 1787, and then propounded throughout his later life. It is not too much to say that Madison's belief in the advantages of religious pluralism, more than any other single factor, convinced him of the empirical merit of his theory of the extensive republic. This belief had been tested in the heat of the politico-religious battle as early as 1785, in the contest against religious assessments in Virginia. In a letter to Jefferson in 1785, Madison had noted that "a coalition between them [i.e., religious sects] could alone endanger our religious rights." [1] This sentiment runs throughout Madison's speeches in the Constitutional Convention, his *Federalist* papers, his letters to Jefferson, and his speeches in the Virginia Ratifying Convention. In the Virginia Ratifying Convention, for example, Madison had declared: "If there were a majority of one sect, a bill of rights would be a poor protection for liberty. Happily for the states, they enjoy the utmost freedom of religion. This freedom arises from that multiplicity of sects, which pervades America, and which is the best and only security for religious liberty in any society. For where there is such a variety of sects, there cannot be a majority of any one sect to oppress and persecute the rest." [2]

"The same security," he wrote to Jefferson, "seems requisite for the civil as for the religious rights of individuals. If the same sect form a majority and have the power, other sects will be sure to be depressed." Madison was apparently aware of the broader application of the idea of a multiplicity of interests as early as 1785. At this date, and in the context of soothing Spain's fears about U.S. expansion in the American

West, he had noted the difficulties for concerted American action attendant upon the multiplication of American settlements: "And as the wills multiply, so will the chances against a dangerous union of them. We experience every day the difficulty of drawing thirteen States into the same plans. Let the number be doubled and so will the difficulty. In the multitude of our Counsellors, Spain may be told, lies her safety." [3]

But if Madison was, in his own fashion, a political pluralist, he was not a pluralist committed to the view that public policy should be the brute resultant of group pressures. He did not and could not endorse the view that somehow all will come out right if many interests struggle for power in the body politic. There were limits to the principle of safety in the number and clash of interests. Somehow, Madison felt, the struggle for power must be regulated and controlled in the public interest. If pluralism was the empirical reality, a neutral sovereign able to advance the public interest was, at least in 1787, the normative hope. Such a sovereign, above the battle, would presumably guide the clash of interests in the interest of the nation. But where was such a neutral sovereign? And in its absence, how could one maintain the common good in a pluralistic society composed of conflicting interests and operating in a governmental system based on the republican principle of majority rule? This, in modern terms, was Madison's problem in 1787. Since many of these interests Madison deemed factional—and since the concept bulks so large in his political theory—we must now examine more fully his diagnosis of faction, the omnipresent and sometimes fatal disease of republican government.

"The instability, injustice, and confusion introduced" by faction "into the public councils," Madison wrote, "have, in truth, been the mortal diseases under which popular governments have everywhere perished." Madison defined faction, it will be remembered, as a "number of citizens, whether amounting to a majority or minority of the whole, who are united and actuated by some common impulse of passion, or of interest, adverse to the rights of other citizens, or to the permanent and aggregate interests of the community." [4]

Because the notion of faction has been held to be imprecise, ambiguous, lacking in empirical stigmata, and therefore operationally useless, it may be helpful here, before we go on, to identify three meanings of faction: faction operating within the state legislatures to impair private rights; faction in the states operating to limit, curtail, weaken, and infect the government of the Union; and faction in actual control of the central government. In 1787 Madison's great concern was faction in the first two senses. Faction in the third sense did not become a clear and present danger until the 1790s.

Why, then, was faction, as thus understood in 1787, so significant for republican theorists? Here Madison emphasized that the difficulty posed by faction was more serious in a republic than in other forms of government because a republic was committed to the protection of the causes of faction. A republic was obligated to respect liberty, and "the diversity in the faculties of man." And as it was unwise to destroy liberty, it was impossible to give "to every citizen the same opinions, the same passions, and the same interests." Free man, "diverse" man, fallible, heterogeneous, heterodox, opinionated, quarrelsome man was then the raw material of faction. The most "common and durable" (but not the only) source of factions Madison traced to the "various and unequal distribution of property." Thus, the ever likely danger of abuse of power—or of injustice—possible in all governments was rooted in the very nature of man and in his behavior. This behavior was especially influenced by the varying ways men went about earning a living. And the men involved were not— on the record—angels or philosopher-kings. They were egoistic seekers after power whose worst qualities were accentuated in a crowd.[5]

Furthermore, elected officials and the electorate did not necessarily stand as guardians of the public weal. For example, of the three motives that guided the decisions of a political candidate—ambition, personal interest, and the public good—the first two were unhappily "proved by experience to be the most prevalent." And, unfortunately, succeeding elections did not throw unscrupulous politicians out of office. "A still more fatal if not more frequent cause" of injustice lies among the people themselves, who, not being sufficiently

107

restrained by enlightened self-interest, respect for character, or religion, were prone to form factional majorities. The result was that "measures are too often decided, not according to the rules of justice and the rights of the minor party, but by the superior force of an interested and overbearing majority." Such would almost always be the case when a powerful faction acts as a judge (in the legislature) in disputes to which the said faction is a party. So ran Madison's diagnosis of faction in 1787. Such a penetrating diagnosis of faction had hitherto been rarely forthcoming from a thoroughly republican thinker.[6]

How, then, was it possible to "secure the public good and private rights against the danger of ... faction, and at the same time to preserve the spirit and the form of popular government"? This was the central question raised by Madison's diagnosis of faction. This formulation alone—too frequently ignored by political theorists enamored of Hobbes' deadly logic, Locke's superb common sense, or Rousseau's paradoxical rhetoric—entitles Madison to enter into the first rank of modern political theorists. Madison's answer to this crucial query constitutes one of the great contributions to republican theory in the modern world. A proper answer was "the greatest desideratum by which this form of government can be rescued from the opprobrium under which it has so long laboured, and be recommended to the esteem and adoption of mankind." [7]

Madison clearly recognized that "there *must* be different interests and parties in society." Homogeneity of interests, opinions, and feelings was impossible. Consequently, the "causes of faction" cannot be removed. Therefore, "relief is only to be sought in the means of controlling its *effects.*" In the Constitutional Convention, Madison had fought hard for a federal "negative" which would counter the danger of disunion that was so frequently engendered by faction within the states. With the defeat of this favored proposal, Madison now had to develop more fully other concepts relating to the control of the effects of faction. Madison argued that minority faction could normally be controlled by the republican principle of majority rule. In defense against faction, he did not fall back upon minority rule based either on force, birth, money, or other non-republican principles. Implicit in his view was the important assumption of a working constitutional order. This assumption was really two-fold. First, Madison assumed that in a republican government decisions would normally be made by a majority of those participating in an election or a legislative vote. Second, he assumed that this majority decision would normally be compatible with basic republican rights and the public interest. The second assumption, as it related to the central government, Madison was to explore more fully in the controversy over the Alien and Sedition Acts. In 1787 the real and pressing danger was majority faction in the states. Here the clue to control was to be found in one of two means. Majority faction could be controlled either by preventing the "existence of the same passion or interest in a majority at the same time," or by rendering such a majority "unable to concert and carry into effect schemes of oppression." [8]

Madison's fear of faction in 1787 was not primarily a fear that part of a republican community would impose its will upon the overwhelming majority, but a dread that the overwhelming majority would unjustly impose its will on the part. This constituted a real predicament for one who was committed as a republican both to majority rule and to justice. It would be misleading to conclude from this that Madison was opposed to democracy as it is understood today. He was opposed to "pure democracy," by which he meant "a society consisting of a small number of citizens, who assemble and administer the government in person. . . ." Pure democracy, he argued, "can admit of no cure for the mischiefs of faction." However, republican or representative government "opens a different prospect, and promises the cure for which we are seeking." [9] The government under the Articles of Confederation was not, of course, a pure democracy either. Madison was deliberately juxtaposing "pure democracy" and republican or representative government. He did so not because there was to be a shift from a pure democratic confederation to a representative republican federal union, but to emphasize that the answer to the problem of faction was not "more democracy" but a differently conceived republic. It is ironic that Madison's very insight into the cancerous elements of his own republican philosophy has led some to doubt that he was a full-fledged republican at all. What did he say?

"The friend of popular governments never finds himself so much alarmed for their character and fate, as when he contemplates their propensity to this dangerous vice [of faction]. He will not fail, therefore, to set a due value on any plan which, without violating the principles to which he is attached, provides a proper cure for it." [10]

Something must be done about the effects of faction, which "continue to be the favorite and fruitful topics from which the adversaries to liberty derive their most specious declamations." [11]

"In the extent and proper structure of the Union, therefore, we behold a *republican* remedy for the diseases most incident to republican government. And according to the degree of pleasure and pride we feel in being *republicans,* ought to be our zeal in cherishing the spirit and supporting the character of Federalists." [12] [Emphasis added.]

Those who view Madison's republicanism as protective coloration to deceive the masses, or as subtle propaganda concealing a philosophy of class and economic exploitation, or as a narrow defense of Southern and agrarian interests, need to reexamine Madison's thought and action with less jaundiced eyes. Madison's motivation was not hitched up to his own economic self-interest, that of his own class, that of his section, or that of the "four groups of personality interests" which, according to Charles Beard, "had been adversely affected under the Articles of Confederation: money, public securities, manufactures, and trade and shipping." Instead, it was based upon a genuine desire to advance the experiment of the federal republic. [13]

One can, then, readily admit that Madison was seeking to conserve something in his battle against faction. He sought to preserve the values, principles, and institutions of republicanism. Of these three, such values as the rights of men were primary and unalterable. Such basic principles as representative, responsible government and majority rule were fundamental too, although they must be viewed realistically in terms of their ability to protect and advance the rights of men. Furthermore, such new principles as federalism might have to be worked out in order that theory might be adjusted both to the maintenance of rights and to the harsh realities of American experience as revealed, for example, by the state of disunion under the Articles of Confederation. Similarly, such institutions as legislative bodies, the courts, and the executive would not lightly be abandoned, although changes in their makeup and operation might become necessary to facilitate the preservation of republicanism. Madison was an advocate of policies designed to conserve these values, principles, and institutions. Only if we understand the nature of this conservatism can we do justice to his theory of faction and, indeed, to his entire political theory.

III

What was the "different prospect" which promised a cure for majority faction? Let us in this section first state and then appraise each of Madison's arguments. In brief, Madison's answer was an extensive, representative, federal republic, operating directly upon the individuals in the union, functioning under a constitution armed with requisite powers of governance, denying certain powers to the states, resting upon a diverse and fundamentally capable electorate, and utilizing the principle of separation of powers.

Madison maintained that an *extensive republic,* a republic embracing a large area and a great number of interests, would more effectively safeguard the rights of citizens and the public interest. This would be so because the multiplicity, diversity, and conflict of factional interests, plus their large sphere of operations, diminished the possibility of factional agreement and unified factional action. The sphere involved must be one "of mean extent." "As in too small a sphere oppressive combinations may be too easily formed against the weaker party; so in too extensive a one, a defensive concert may be rendered too difficult against the oppression of those entrusted with the administration." Madison's concept of what was "a sphere of mean extent" was, however, quite generous. It enabled him later to see the growth of the West as an ally in the battle against faction. The addition of Western states would constitute a further enlargement of the republic. Although this aspect of Madison's theory was no-where fully articulated, he did note that the growth of the West would not make the republic too extensive because the construction of roads, canals, and other improvements in communication would serve to unite the expanding nation.[14]

Madison's argument on behalf of the extensive republic is still largely true. The number, complexity, and competition of the interests and pressures at work in America have cer-tainly operated in large measure to protect private rights and the public interest. Private rights can be defined concretely in terms of such basic matters as religious freedom, freedom of speech and assembly, protection of private property, and the right to vote, among other rights. And the public interest can be defined in terms of a rough policy-balance among contend-ing democratic interests. These definitions may not be perfect, but they do have an operational validity. As Madison cor-rectly saw, the prospect of safety in numbers and size would be as true in politics as in religion. Interests compete and conflict with each other, and this obstructs steamroller tech-niques. Furthermore, geography accentuates diversity, even within a major economic division, as for example in the field of agriculture. In addition, sectionalism to some extent mili-tates against national concert by even the same interests. Then, too, the very size of some interests, as in the case of a national labor, farm, or business organization, leads not to monolithic unity but to internal strife and division as rival leaders employ real or invented differences to advance their own special ends. Furthermore, the very nature of democratic politics—the appeal for financial, organizational, or electoral support—frequently requires the varying interests to join po-litical coalitions, to enter into political compromises, and to tone down extravagant demands in order to push the major items on their own agenda. What is too often forgotten is that the party process not only restrains the parties, as they re-spond to the innumerable minorities that make up a winning electoral and legislative coalition in a given campaign or on a given issue, but also the interests themselves, as they too must make concessions to advance their own central goals. It is, of course, saying too much to argue that Madison saw all this or stated it in this fashion. The point is that the extensive republic does act to take the edge off extremism in politics. It militates against gross imbalance. And to the extent that factions illustrate both extremism and imbalance, Madison wrought better than he knew.

On the other hand, it is also true that certain modern developments have facilitated greater economic concert of operation and hence have functioned in part to reduce the present validity of Madison's eighteenth century point. These developments include nationwide parties, modern pressure groups, modern media of rapid and mass communication, giant corporations and trade unions and—frequently working through all these agencies—the pervasive unifying power of economic wealth or ideology.[15] However, second thoughts are in order in connection with the technological developments which seemingly operate to constrict Madison's extensive republic and to increase the feasibility of factional agreement and unified factional action. For if the nation has become smaller and communication is easier, the number of interests has grown and the conflicts among interests have by no means abated. Hence, some interests may use the same means of communication to oppose alleged factional groups that the groups may use to unite and act. And if parties can act as advocates of alleged factional ends, so, too, they can and do serve as mediators among factional interests. In this way they may restrain, control, even educate factions in their struggle for power. This insight about parties cannot be attributed as such to Madison, who, after all, was writing at a time when parties were infants and in disrepute as factions. However, it is to Madison's credit that he came to distinguish between party and faction and came to see the necessity and desirability of parties, rightly understood, acting to check factional power, mediating among factional struggles, advancing what he held to be the right republican notions.[16]

On balance, then, if modern technology and modern politics have reduced the effectiveness of Madison's initial argument, they have in a certain sense enlarged the number of interests at work, equipped anti-factional interests with means for combating faction, and produced in the modern political party an agency for harmonizing to some extent the frequently discordant demands of the heterogeneous coalitions

113

that make up the modern political party. These factors work in all fifty states. In some, however, they are less noticeable than in others. Strikingly, it has been the one-dominant-interest state which has been generally characterized as most subject to factional mischief. Historically, for example, the dominant interest of all Southern states in maintaining segregation is a modern illustration of the force of Madison's argument, assuming that segregation in the public schools is contrary to private rights and the public interest. A multiplicity of politically powerful minorities, on the other hand, makes for their self-protection, even if their strategic location in the big cities in the populous states often enhances their political power beyond their more rightful claim in terms of sheer number.

Representative government was another major concept serving to explain how the effects of faction could be controlled. Madison was by no means blind to the possibility that "Men of factious tempers, of local prejudices, or of sinister designs, may, by intrigue, by corruption, or by any other means, first obtain the suffrages, and then betray the interests, of the people." But he believed that an extensive republic is more likely to produce the "election of proper guardians of the public weal" than a "small" republic. To Madison this was true for at least two reasons. First, the extensive republic, having a large population, would normally have more fit men potentially capable of representing it; and this larger number of potential representatives would ensure a "greater probability of a fit choice." Secondly, the greater number of citizens in the "extensive republic" would, in comparison with the process in a small republic, make it "more difficult for unworthy candidates to practice with success the vicious arts by which elections are too often carried." A representative system indirectly expressing the popular will, sometimes twice removed, would presumably filter out factional passion and retain only the public interest. Such representative government thus provided that purified and ennobled "process of elections" which would "refine and enlarge the public view." The representative was not to be a rubber stamp of the electorate. He had a republican obligation to consider their wishes, but he was not bound to follow their wishes. He must follow his own judgment of what the public interest required. He must not truckle to the mob. He must not be carried away by popular passion. He had, then, not only an obligation to represent the wishes of his constituency, but a more important obligation to abide by higher standards of republican representation. These standards required him to think for himself and to consider the aggregate interests of the community in addition to those of his constituency.[17]

Theoretically, the first of Madison's two reasons for believing that an extensive republic is more likely to produce the election of proper representatives than a small republic is well taken *if* one disregards or ignores some important aspects of political life. One must disregard the distaste or disinclination for public life which weighs heavily on many of those who are fit. One must ignore such other realistic facts of political life as the role of the inner party in selecting candidates, the doctrine of availability, the lust for victory regardless of decent political ethics. These factors do not completely destroy the validity of Madison's point, but they certainly limit its force. Madison's second reason also seems well taken when we consider the relatively better caliber of those in the Senate than in the House and in the Presidency than in Congress. In most cases the broader constituency makes for a broader outlook in the candidate, even though the person may not be a superior individual.

Yet considering the demagogues who have graced or disgraced the Senate, and noting the advantages that the modern demagogue and unscrupulous candidate have to deceive a larger electorate, Madison's reasoning must not be accepted without important qualifications. Does a representative system purify the electoral process? Does it filter out the passion and self-interest of politics? Here one lacks convincing empirical evidence that might prove or disprove this Madisonian proposition. Nevertheless, knowledge of the technique of representation as it functions in a republic enables one to state that it can and does have these effects, although it would be false to say that it has these effects in all cases. One is plagued here by the difficulty of defining what is meant by the term "purify" and "faction." However, insofar as a representative system enhances thoughtful deliberation, rational

115

debate, and consideration of a broader range of interests, it may be said to purify and filter the passions of politics. It would be presumptuous to contend that the filter always works or always works well. Elections frequently accentuate self-interest, aggravate the passions, and bring the worst not the best to the top. Ultimately, the technique of representation is often only as good as the sense and sobriety of the citizens who are to be represented or, more accurately, of the active political minority who concern themselves with public affairs.

Finally, what is to be said of Madison's Burkean notion of the role of the representative? Does the representative exercise independent judgment as he listens to debate, harkens to the wishes of specific interests on specific issues, reflects on the general undefined sentiment in his constituency, weighs the appeals of President, party leaders and legislative colleagues, and prudently attempts to pursue his own conception of the public interest? If he does so, he will personally act as a filter against faction. This, however, is a large *if;* and although more balancing of this kind goes on than the cynical political observer is willing to admit, there can be no doubt that few representatives can adhere for long to such an exalted standard of public duty. Too often the representative finds it all too easy to disguise faction in the robes of the public interest, to identify self-interest and the common interest, and to succumb to the understandable desire for reelection. He may succumb, of course, on philosophical grounds of adhering to the democratic will of his constituents or of not sacrificing his office and his long-term ability to do good in order to maintain temporarily a broader and more ethical position. In brief, then, Madison's arguments based upon a representative system provide only partial grounds for believing in the efficacy of this system in controlling the effects of faction.

Madison also held that a strengthened *federal form of government* would serve to guard against factional evil. This advantage was implicit in the very concept of an invigorated, extensive republic whose conflicting interests and greater powers, size, number and variety of interests made it more difficult for state factions to corrupt and disrupt the government of the union. This advantage was also implicit in a "partly federal and partly national" system. In such a system the division of power minimized the prize of national factional victory, and the compartmentalization of power rendered other states in the union, and the union itself, less vulnerable to factional contagion. Moreover, in such a system the states would act as watchdogs "to detect or to defeat a conspiracy" by the central government "against the liberty of their common constituents." [18]

In *The Federalist,* Madison retained many of his earlier high nationalistic hopes. The central government, even though it was organized on the federal principle, would have plenty of power—positively to govern and negatively to bind the factional elements in the states. However, the failure of some of Madison's high nationalistic proposals left the states with more and the nation with less power than Madison preferred. The consequence of this historical development for Madison's theory of faction was its undeniable negativism. In 1787 this negativism as it weakened the central government vis-á-vis the states was unwanted. In 1787 Madison did not see that the same difficulties that face a factional minority or majority might also face a rightful minority or majority. Thus, according to Madison's theory, legislation in the public interest as well as legislation opposed to the public interest would be blocked. In pressing for due supremacy in 1787 Madison apparently felt that there would be no obstacle to the exercise of national power on behalf of the national interest, once the central government achieved needed substantive powers and the states were put in their proper places in the federal system. Madison's unstated assumption was that rightful majorities in the new, strengthened, federal, extensive republic would normally have their way. [19]

However, the difficulties which have faced the advocates of positive government in the public interest in the late nineteenth and twentieth centuries, and the actuality of unjust coalitions, will cause those who desire to use certain Hamiltonian means to secure certain Jeffersonian ends to be somewhat sceptical of this assumption. Here in the essentially negative aspects of Madison's theory of faction, a negativism rooted both in the notion of the extensive republic and in that

117

of federalism, one finds its chief failing as a viable theory for the present world. The extensive republic, by its very nature, tends to slow up the formation of public policy at both national and state levels. Similarly, federalism slows up the formation and operation of uniform national policy. This might be desirable, for Madison, if the policy was factional policy; but it can hardly be said that he would desire to see sound republican policies obstructed either within the states, between states, or throughout the Union.

The nationalistic vision that Madison brought to the Convention had already been impaired by political developments within the Convention. It was further limited in his defense of the Constitution in *The Federalist*. And it was to be badly dimmed by his reaction to Federalist policy in the 1790s. What Madison forgot when he developed his theory of the extensive republic was that triumph over faction was only one half of the republican triumph. The republican ascendency could not be fully assured until Republicans were in control of all governments in the Union and were using their skills to advance the national interest as they conceived it. However, by the time the Republicans came to power in 1800, Madison was already so impressed by the ideological weapons which he had forged in the 1790s to blast the Federalists that he was unable to abandon them and recapture anew the positive nationalistic spirit of the spring, summer, and fall of 1787. In political context, this is understandable. Today, however, this failure limits the relevance of Madison's theory for those who favor a broad exercise of national power in what they hold to be the national interest. For those who are unconcerned about the exercise of such power, or who favor the obstruction of national power, the negative aspects of a federal republic are indeed welcome.

Another major ingredient in Madison's theory of control was *requisite powers of governance.* The expanded and invigorated powers which were necessary to establish the due supremacy of the central government also constituted an "enlargement" of the republic. In this way the republic became "extensive" in its powers as well as in larger size and greater number of interests. With the expansion of the powers of the central government, the focus of power on many issues would shift from the states, where factional majorities had a relatively easier time of accomplishing their objectives, to the central government, where the difficulty of factional triumph would be in direct proportion to the size of the country and the number of interests at work. This is the only logical answer explaining why the government under the Constitution would be any more of an "extensive republic"—in geographic size, number, and variety of interests, and, therefore, give any better protection against the effects of faction—than the government under the Articles of Confederation. This relatively neglected point, though perhaps not succinctly stated in Madison's writings, is implicit in his arguments based upon the theory of the extensive republic. In at least one place in Number 10 *Federalist,* Madison suggested the point when he indicated that "the great and aggregate interests" are "referred to the national, the local and particular to the State legislatures." Thus faction would be stymied in its efforts to corrupt and disrupt "the great and aggregate interests" of the nation.[20]

The modern critic, with the advantage of hindsight, might feel that Madison underemphasized the ability of faction to gain active control of the national government and its expanded and invigorated powers. Such control would challenge a basic premise of Madison's theory. Madison hoped that a purified and ennobled electoral system, plus the other political, social, and economic restraints on faction in an extensive republic, would produce legislators capable of resisting faction, capable of keeping their eyes focused on the national interest. His hopes were to prove ill-founded in the 1790s. Then he was brought face-to-face with the problem of faction in active control at the national level. This disturbing reality later forced Madison to develop more fully his concept of republican opposition. This concept was a necessary theoretical development without which the theory of the extensive republic could be severely and adversely criticized.

A more obvious factor facilitating the control of faction was *constitutional prohibition,* particularly certain restrictions on the power of the states. Most important in this regard was the injunction of Article 1, Section 10: "No state shall . . . emit bills of credit; make anything but gold and silver a legal tender in payment of debts; pass any ... law impairing the obligation of contracts. ..." To these prohibitions one must add those which prohibited the states from entering into treaties, taxing imports or exports, or in general violating the federal Constitution or obstructing federal laws. All these prohibitions had been adumbrated in the "Vices." Madison strongly felt that the very character of a republican government—its reputation for justice, stability, and good faith—required these constitutional bulwarks against faction.[21]

An adversely critical attitude toward protections afforded property rights has made some observers forget that those protections relating to property may be defended for different reasons. They may be defended by those having a selfish interest in the maintenance of the propertied status quo. But they may also be defended by those, like Madison, who are concerned with the preservation of "the first principles of the social compact and ... every principle of sound legislation." To appreciate fully Madison's republican endorsement of these constitutional prohibitions, one must appraise them in the broader light shed by such little-read literature as his essay "Property" and his penetrating criticism of Jefferson's doctrine of the continuing majority. Writing in the natural law tradition, Madison held that wise and just government must respect a property in rights as well as a right of property. Similarly, one must concede that both rest upon a certain amount of foresight and permanence in the affairs of the generations of man.[22]

In assessing Madison's solution to the problem of controlling the self-destructive features of republican government, one must also consider the more optimistic side of his appraisal of political man. Madison was no blind and uncritical admirer of the sovereign capacity of the people. Nevertheless, he early believed and never lost the conviction that a *diverse and fundamentally capable electorate* was the prime safeguard of republican institutions. Despite his emphatic recognition of the need for "auxiliary precautions," he firmly maintained that a "dependence on the people is ... the primary control on the government," a people whose social and economic diversity militated against single-minded agreement and action, a people whose agreement on fundamentals served to underwrite the calculated risk of majority rule.[23]

Madison's qualified confidence in a republican people is a calculated risk that he felt was operationally valid. We will return again to this point in the next chapter. Here we need only note that the success of republican institutions has, in part at least, rested upon the good sense of the republic's citizens.

Separation of powers would provide yet another safeguard against factional abuse of power. Most important here was a wise and stable Senate which would operate to check abuses stemming either from the "various and interfering" factional interests in the states or from the national government itself, should it set "up an interest adverse to that of the whole Society." The branches of government must, however, be sufficiently connected to permit mutual "constitutional control" and mutual self-protection.[24]

One cannot blink the fact that Madison viewed a wise, virtuous, and stable Senate as an anchor of the ship of state, particularly as an anchor that would protect property against factional storms. Nor can one deny that he looked upon the presidency as an organ that would operate to "prevent popular or factious injustice." And we may assume that he shared Hamilton's views in Number 78 *Federalist* on the Supreme Court's role as a protector of basic individual rights against factional infringements. However, too much can be made of the cardinal importance of separation of powers or of Madison's fears of factional mischief in the lower legislative body. Too often, critics have forgotten that Madison was more concerned with faction operating in the state legislatures than faction working in the national House of Representatives. Separation of powers was not the primary component of Madison's theory of faction and certainly not the key principle of his entire political theory. It was clearly not an original Madisonian contribution as the concept of the extensive republic was.[25]

Here a related point can be made. In Madison's theory, the Senate, the President, and the Supreme Court were not to operate as plutocratic or selfishly aristocratic organs guarding vested property interests against the democratic majority.

They were to protect property against factional actions. Yet the property to be so defended is not to be identified with corporate wealth and/or monopoly, with a permanently entrenched status quo, or even exclusively with tangible property. There is no mistake more profound than identifying Madison's views toward property in particular and toward conservatism in general with those of Hamilton, Fisher Ames, and Calhoun or with that of such later laissez-faire conservatives as Sumner, Field, and Carnegie in the post-Civil War "Age of Enterprise." It is then a serious mistake to contend that Madison envisaged the President, the Senate, and the Court as guarding only the classes against the masses or even the rich and wellborn against the poor and and ill-born. As Madison never tired of insisting, the rich could oppress the poor, the poor could injure the rich, merchants could harm farmers, and farmers could damage merchants. Faction could cut many ways.[26]

Separation of powers was only one factor that Madison relied upon in his efforts to control the effects of faction. And it was by no means the most important one. As Number 51 *Federalist*—the last of five essays on separation of powers—makes clear, if one had to single out one factor as the most important, one would have to stress the notion of the extensive republic—large size and diverse and multiple interests—as the cardinal factor that would operate to curb factional activities. This is not a formal and constitutional factor. It is not formally spelled out in the Constitution that there are multiple and diverse interests in America, functioning in a large geographical area made so by the Constitution. The larger sphere constitutes the natural geographical area in which interests naturally operate. However, the effectiveness of these factors of size, multiplicity, and diversity is undoubtedly enchanced by the constitutional division of powers between nation and states, by separation of powers, by representation, and by specific constitutional powers and prohibitions. Without the larger sphere, and multiple and diverse interests, all the formal constitutional factors might not work. With them, together with the sound sense of a diverse republican electorate, the extensive republic has a greater opportunity to control faction.

In treating Madison's theory of faction, two other neglected factors, closely related to all the foregoing points, must be examined. One of these relates to Madison's concept of the "neutral sovereign," the other to suffrage. The omissions of a "neutral sovereign" and a severely restricted suffrage from Madison's theory were not accidental.

First, what of Madison's views of the "neutral sovereign"? Madison's concept of the "neutral sovereign" calls attention to his early recognition of the necessity for a dispassionate, disinterested, and just judge to settle disputes among contending factions. Perhaps he never fully developed this idea because it is subject to potent criticism stemming from his own dynamic political premises. Hamilton recognized at the time of the Constitutional Convention that if factions struggle for power in the union and if the union is republican, the sovereign cannot be neutral or cannot easily remain neutral. Sovereign power must either reflect the will of one faction or another, reflect the public interest, try to maintain a balance amid conflicting interests, or do nothing. Madison was less quick to grasp this. He wanted his "neutral sovereign" to reflect and advance the public interest. Yet he recognized the danger of a sovereign will allegedly reflecting the public interest but actually independent of the will of the community. Perhaps it was for this reason that he dropped further elaboration of the concept. Instead, he fell back on the idea that the public interest can best be advanced if government recognizes its affirmative role as one very significant contender amid the struggle of contending interests. Unfortunately, this point, which was apparently Madison's potential solution, was not fully developed in his writings. When, in the 1790s, Madison again became aware of the national government's positive role, it was in connection with Federalist policy which he deemed factional! It is, however, interesting to speculate on how this concept of the "neutral sovereign" might have developed but for Madison's subsequent reaction to the Hamiltonian program. There is some evidence to support the hypothesis that the President might have filled the role of Madison's "neutral sovereign." Before his fight against Hamilton, before he wrote the "Helvidius" letters in which he criticized the President's discretion on the issue of neutrality in the Franco-British conflict then raging, Madison strongly supported the independence of the Chief Executive within his sphere. During his tenure in high office he held to a similar view. He particularly sought scope for the Executive in foreign affairs. These views are in accord with his view of the presidency in the Constitutional Convention. There, it may be remembered, he had looked upon the President as one who would act for the nation, for the whole people, and not for a sectional or factional part of the nation.[27]

The idea of the "neutral sovereign" is based upon the possibility of an organization of government capable of advancing the public interest. An underlying assumption is that there is a public interest and that it can be identified, and hence followed by someone like the President. Madison never subjected this assumption to the kind of analysis it has undergone in modern times. His belief in the public interest is a faith ultimately grounded in his natural law orientation. There must be, he implied, a conception of justice, of the public good, of the national interest in society and government, that can be known to a rational man of goodwill. Madison's failure to probe the meaning of these terms may very well have prevented him from developing the idea of the "neutral sovereign." Certainly this failure tends to leave his remedy for faction very much up in the air. How could one really be sure that a given interest was a faction? What would guide the "neutral sovereign" in allowing only right interests to be advanced? According to what objective standard would the government regulate and control the various interfering interests in society? If the public interest and faction cannot be defined objectively, how can factional tyranny be controlled? If people may act to control what they deem to be faction, how can they be sure that they are right? If it is possible to assume consensus on what is and what is not faction, what happens when political conflict reveals no such general consensus? At first glance, these seem to be devastating questions.

On a second glance, however, one may uncover some implied answers in Madison's writings. Madison would have probably replied that one must fall back on the operation of a majority-rule system as the best possible alternative in a republican society.[28] One must assume that the logic, objective fruits, and future consequences of certain alleged factional policies will be so clearly contrary to the people's accepted notions of justice, the common good, and the national interest that the majority may *feel* right on the basis of both republican logic and common experience in acting to counter faction. Can one, however, go beyond this answer, which is by no means satisfactory? The best one can do, Madison would have responded, is to seek to strengthen the underlying consensus, the agreement on enough fundamentals, to hold a civilized society and an orderly government together. In this endeavor, greatest emphasis must be placed upon the most basic rights: freedom of conscience, speech, press, assembly, and the right to vote. Beyond this, one can only stress the prudential value of justice, the common good, the national interest, and indicate their pragmatic relationship to generally accepted ends. These ends involve such matters as the protection of individual and group rights, orderly resolution of disputes, and confidence in civilized life. One can also insist that the rejection of such operative-ideals will lead to alternatives that are objectively obnoxious according to the testimony of most civilized men. To note Madison's belief in the public interest is to concede that his theory of faction is normatively prejudiced. It was, indeed, part of his republican ideology. But this concession does not mean that such ideology has no relation to empirical reality. Madison's theory may not be scientifically operational in modern terms. But if one assumes that men like Madison can give their own specific definitions to faction, then it is possible to do the following:

—To see if the factional forces in the states seeking the printing of depreciated paper money could get together and either (1) prevent the central government from adopting a sound money policy or (2) continue paper emissions in the states, to the degradation of the public credit.

—To ascertain if the factional opponents of an adequate and reliable national revenue could unite and obstruct the central government in acquiring tax monies for necessary national purposes.

—To note if the factional opponents of more uniform national commercial policies could join forces and defeat the national government's efforts to work out a more uniform national policy on commercial matters.

These are selected examples only. Madison could and did give concrete and objective meaning to such terms as "tyranny," "natural rights," and "permanent and aggregate interests of the community." Not all would agree with his meanings; but once his definitions are accepted, theory becomes operationally meaningful. Madison's theory consequently takes on the form of an "If ... then ..." proposition. *If* advocates of paper money constitute a faction, *then* Madison's theory of the extensive republic does or does not operate to control such faction. In this sense, Madison's theory is operational even within the framework of modern empirical political theory.

However, the ideological battle over the definition of faction persists and, like the comparable battle over the good life, will persist so long as man remains the free creature he is. Wisdom consists in candidly recognizing that this battle will never be resolved scientifically. The best one can do is to demonstrate the empirical consequences that flow from the acceptance of one definition or another. This denial of the possibility of objectively and scientifically demonstrating the empirical truth of normative judgments does not mean that normative belief must be abandoned or that such judgments have no relationship to empirical reality. Belief in such judgments arises from and is definitely related to human experience. Such beliefs constitute practical wisdom. Such wisdom is a fact of life even though it cannot be measured scientifically.

What of Madison's views on suffrage? More specifically, what is the relationship of Madison's views of suffrage to his theory of faction? Madison resisted the temptation to curb faction by curbing suffrage. This followed from his explicit recognition that faction was not a monopoly of the poor, illborn, unpropertied masses and that a restriction of the right of suffrage was unmistakably anti-republican. This does not mean that Madison in 1787 or 1828 was, practically speaking, a modern democrat on the question of suffrage. He was not in his lifetime an advocate even of universal white male suffrage, let alone a believer in the right to vote for all, including

Blacks and women. Yet he did not build his theory of faction on the basis of a restricted suffrage. And he did recognize that in the last analysis the rights of persons must take priority over the rights of property. Madison, who was fearful of a propertyless majority oppressing a propertied minority, also recognized that the reverse was possible. The rights of both persons and property must be protected. A compromise solution, giving each a defensive constitutional posture, was desirable but perhaps not politically feasible. And if one must bow to the feasible and the ultimate logic of the electoral partnership of power, most of the features of the extensive republic would operate to cushion the effects of universal suffrage, as this posed a potential threat of majority faction.[29]

There can be no doubt that Madison was troubled by the question of suffrage throughout his life. In the Philadelphia Convention he had expressed a preference for a freehold suffrage—suffrage based on the ownership of landed property. According to Douglass Adair, Madison's agrarian predilections constituted the inarticulate major premise of his theory of faction. Yet Madison was also fearful of an abridgment of the right of suffrage because this was the way "Aristocracies have been built on the ruins of popular government." Madison wanted to maintain a relatively broad suffrage. He was also disposed prudently to support what was feasible. Although he noted that the propertyless majority constituted a danger to the rights of property and liberty, he also observed the greater probability that the rich and ambitious might use the propertyless multitude to advance their own dangerous ends. He explicitly stated that the potentially adverse effects of universal suffrage might be cushioned by a number of factors. They might be cushioned by large electoral districts for one of the two legislative branches, by longer terms of office for one branch, by "the ordinary influence possessed by property," by "the superior information incident to its holders," by "the popular sense of justice enlightened and enlarged by a diffusive education," and by "the difficulty of combining and effectuating unjust purposes throughout an extensive country." Thus it was that Madison relied upon his theory of the extensive republic and not upon a restricted suffrage to curb majority faction. Theoretically, republican theory required the broadening of the partnership of power. Despite their personal preference for a compromise that would guard both the rights of persons and the rights of property, republicans must ultimately guard against republican faction by relying upon the safeguards offered by the extensive republic.[30]

Madison's position is one that will not endear him to the heart of either the modern democrat or anti-democrat. As is so often true in his case, his position does not lend itself to easy slogans. Perhaps for this reason, Americans have never had a Madison Day Dinner! Madison's position is complex. Madison is more likely to appeal to the critical mind which respects the rights of persons but is not convinced of the people's omnipotence, omniscience, or flawless devotion to the public interest. He will appeal to those who respect the rights of property but only because property, rightfully employed, contributes to liberty, productiveness, and order.

IV

Madison did more than state, if he did less than solve, the problem of faction. The problem of faction is insoluble in the world as it is. All that one can do is mitigate the evils of faction. This, however, is a great deal. Here Madison pointed the way. He first called our attention to the explanation of the several ways by which these evils might be mitigated. His solution is not perfect, final, or pat. Still he grappled bravely and creatively with the self-destructive features of republican government which were, he brilliantly emphasized, rooted in human freedom. It is a tribute to Madison's theoretical genius that he could turn the supposed vices of a large state into the redeeming virtues of an extensive republic. The operation of a multiplicity of interests, instead of making for confusion and chaos, instead of preventing the attainment of the proper standard of the public interest, may to some extent safeguard justice against perversion. The extensive republic, of course, creates problems of its own, particularly the problem of achieving effective positive government, necessary national uniformity, and republican harmony amid republican diversity. Yet it has functioned with a moderate degree of success. Americans today know what no one knew in 1787. They know that republican government in a large state need not succumb to republican factionalism. For the political theory explaining the workability of republican government in a large country, modern democracy owes Madison an intellectual debt which has never been fully and adequately acknowledged.

CHAPTER 6

The Anti-Republican Danger
and Democratic Politics

> "... It is proper to take alarm at the first experiment on
> our liberties. We hold this prudent jealousy to be the first duty
> of citizens.... The freemen of America did not wait till
> usurped power had strengthened itself by exercise, and entan-
> gled the question in precedents. They saw all the consequences
> in principle, and they avoided the consequences by denying the
> principle."
>
> — 2 *Writings* 185-186 (1785)
> ("Memorial and Remonstrance
> Against Religious Assessments")

> "Republicans ... must be anxious ... in defending liberty
> against power, and power against licentiousness: and in keep-
> ing every portion of power within its proper limits; by this
> means discomforting the partisans of anti-republican contriv-
> ances."
>
> — 6 *Writings* 85 (1792) ("Charters")

> "... If majority governments ... be the worst of Govern-
> ments[,] those who think and say so cannot be within the pale
> of the republican faith. They must either join the avowed
> disciples of aristocracy, oligarchy or monarchy, or look for a
> Utopia exhibiting a perfect homogeneousness of interests,
> opinions and feelings nowhere yet found in civilized communi-
> ties."
>
> — 9 *Writings* 526 (1833)
> (Memorandum on "Majority Government")

I

Madison's political theory, I have argued in this study,
can best be understood in terms of a response to four major,

interrelated, difficulties that faced a thoroughly republican thinker as he sought to reconcile liberty and large size in the infant American republic. Three of these—disunion, large size, faction—I have dealt with in previous chapters. It now remains to treat more fully a fourth difficulty—the anti-republican danger—which I have touched upon earlier, but which I can now use to illustrate Madison's contribution to a theory of bold republican leadership, of civil liberties, and of a republican political opposition. For the sake of simplicity I shall lump the components of these several theories together and give the amalgamation the title of a theory of democratic politics. This theory is thoroughly democratic insofar as it rests upon the twin premises of popular rule and protection of basic rights. It is a democratic theory, moreover, which seeks to do equal justice to liberty and to power, to freedom and to order. It is democratic, too, in that Madison endorses the principle of equal rights for all and special privileges for none.

I shall argue that ingredients of this theory—involving bold leadership and the protection of basic rights—can be detected during the American Revolution and in the crucial year of 1787. But it was not until the 1790s, with the emergence of the Hamiltonian program, and, then, the Alien and Sedition Acts, that the more clearly democratic character of this theory becomes predominant. At this time, too, Madison develops his ideas of a republican party opposition and makes these ideas a crucial part of what I have called his theory of democratic politics. His views on a republican party opposition, I have already suggested, were essential to the consummation of his theory of the control of faction dominating the national government. A republican party becomes the nationwide instrument to fight against factional control of the central government. Still later in the 1820s and 1830s, Madison employs his theory of democratic politics to fight the advocates of nullification and secession. They, too, threaten not only majority government but genuinely republican union.

In presenting Madison's theory of democratic politics in more systematic form, I should warn the reader that such a theory is not to be found articulated in such a neat fashion in Madison's own writings. I have given form to Madison's thought. However, if the more systematic statement is my own, the raw material that I have drawn upon is Madison's.

The issue that led Madison to articulate what I have called a theory of democratic politics was the question of how to cope with the anti-republican danger. Madison's answer to this question can be briefly summarized as follows: (1) develop a keen analysis of the anti-republican danger and sound the alarm; (2) if possible, seek through political and constitutional debate to defeat dangerous anti-republican measures before passage; (3) rely upon popular protest and party organization—with the help of a free press—to mobilize support for republican purposes; (4) employ orthodox constitutional means—i.e., impeachment, elections, repeal, amendment—to alter public policy; (5) retreat, if necessary, to ultraconstitutional interposition—to the people in the states as the final source of all legitimate constitutional authority; and (6) invoke the moral appeal to revolution which, though outside the framework of constitutional union, is the ultimate appeal by republicans in defense of popular rule and basic rights against intolerable oppression.

Let us now proceed to examine these interrelated points.

II

Analysis of Danger. Madison's general analysis of the anti-republican danger, one that he held throughout his life, can be easily summarized. He held that no republican government could claim political immortality. Degeneration and destruction brought on by enemies within was a constantly threatening disease in all government. A republic was not immune. Government was dynamic and movement was not necessarily upward toward a republican utopia. Anti-republican forces existed, constantly exerted their pressures, and made their appeals. They would exploit republican weakness, inefficiency, abuse of power, and lack of vigilance, and would wield power whenever possible. Consequently, those who would lead in establishing and maintaining a republic must make government strong, effective, and just, and encourage the citizenry to be alert, informed, and virtuous.

As early as 1780, before the American Revolution was over, he had enunciated one of his central political themes summarized above. This theme he expressed in the Congress of the Confederation, the Virginia House of Delegates, the Philadelphia Convention, the Virginia Ratifying Convention, and repeated throughout his life. Anti-republican "innovations," he warned, might be "intruded" unless the government were organized in a just, efficient, and stable way. The republican experiment might be imperiled by those forces that overtly or covertly sought a different brand of government. Consequently, because of the real danger that such men and forces posed for the establishment and maintenance of the republic, the union must be so organized as to blunt their criticism. This is, without doubt, the major factor explaining Madison's determined efforts to strengthen and invigorate the powers of the central government in 1787.[1]

On the floor of the Philadelphia Convention, Madison again spoke directly to this theme: "What we wished was to give to the Government that stability which was everywhere called for, and which the *Enemies of the Republican form alleged to be inconsistent with its nature. . . .* He [Madison was writing of himself in the third person] conceived it to be of great importance that a stable and firm Government organized in the republican form should be held out to the people. If this be not done, and the people be left to judge . . . of the defective systems under which they now live, it is much to be *feared that the time is not distant when in universal disgust, they will renounce the blessing which they have purchased at so dear a rate, and be ready for any change that may be proposed to them."*[2] [Emphasis added.]

And so Madison was ready to act. He had worked hard to shore up the faltering Confederation both in the Congress and in the Virginia House of Delegates. As the failure of limited reforms became apparent, it also became clear that new and bold moves were necessary if the union were to be saved, and anti-republican "intrusions" avoided. Madison had been somewhat reluctant to make such moves earlier, but when the need became imperative his analysis of the danger did not lead him to shrink from firm leadership to effect a major change in the union. The Annapolis Convention was deliberately used to prepare the way for a new constitution. The mere patching of the old govermental fabric would not do.[3] In the Philadelphia Convention, Madison was unequivocal in proposing a new constitution based on new principles. The time was now ripe for action. Such a golden hour might not come again. So strike back boldly!

"My own idea [Madison wrote to Jefferson on September 6, 1787] is, that the public will now, or in a very little time, receive anything that promises stability to the public councils and security to private rights, and that no regard ought to be had to local prejudices or temporary considerations. If the present moment is lost, it is hard to say what may be our fate."[4]

Bold action, justified on the principle of self-preservation, was dictated by Madison's analysis of the danger. And so in *The Federalist*, he set forth the argument justifying the constitutional revolution of 1787. He argued that daring leadership was made necessary by republican theory because republican theory placed self-preservation and the safety of the people above all questions of constitutional legality. He contended that whether the Constitutional Fathers exceeded their powers or not, they were justified, in the interest of the safety and happiness of the American people, in doing what they did.

". . . If they had exceeded their powers, they were not only warranted but required, as the confidential servants of their country, by the circumstances in which they were placed, to exercise the liberty which they assumed; and . . . if they had violated both their powers and their obligations, in proposing a Constitution, this ought nevertheless to be embraced, if it be calculated to accomplish the views and happiness of the people of America."[5]

In brief: in republican politics, danger to the safety of the state and the happiness of the people justified the bold appeal to the constituent power of the people.

Moreover, Madison insisted, substance ought not to be sacrificed to form. The ultimate constituent power of the people, invoked in the Revolution and utilized to establish the constitutions of the states, was the precious right being employed by the Constitutional Fathers. They acted as "patriotic and respectable" leaders on behalf of the people, who could not "spontaneously and universally" "move in concert" to implement the right embodied in the Declaration of Independence—that is, to "abolish or alter their governments as to them shall seem most likely to effect their safety and happiness." The people themselves, through their representatives in special constitutional conventions, would make the final decision on the new constitution. And the "approbation" of "this supreme authority" would "blot out antecedent errors and irregularities." This same argument was used against those who insisted that the Confederation could not be superseded without the unanimous consent of the parties to it. Again, the principle that decided the matter was that of "self-preservation," the "transcendent law of nature and of nature's God, which declares that the safety and happiness of society are the objects at which all political institutions aim, and to which all such institutions must be sacrificed."[6]

Madison's analysis of the danger of a weak and ineffective republican union—as it might lead to a reaction against republicanism—led him to advocate strong leadership in securing a stronger republican union. I have stressed this analysis—and Madison's justification of it—because it helps us to understand better Madison's action in the Virginia Resolutions. The analysis in both instances is fundamentally the same on key points. When the safety and happiness of the people were at stake, Madison's usually high regard for existing legal forms would give way to his insistence upon placing the substance of republican liberty and union ahead of accepted but malfunctioning constitutional or legal forms. Such action would be sanctioned by popular approval. Here we see clearly the continuity between Madison's bold action in defense of the new federal constitution and his bold action against a perversion of republican liberty and union in the 1790s.

To emphasize the continuity of Madison's analysis—and the point that Madison in the period prior to the 1790s was a republican concerned with individual rights as well as with national power—it may be helpful to call to mind again his valiant efforts on behalf of freedom of religious conscience. Here, too, he sought to anticipate the anti-republican danger. Here, too, perhaps he exaggerated the danger. Here, too, moreover, a bold alarm and bold leadership might serve to defeat anti-republican forces before they could effectuate their anti-republican ends. In his 1785 "Memorial and Remonstrance Against Religious Assessments"—a powerful blast at a Virginia bill which required payments by all for the support of the Christian religion—Madison argued that the dominant legislative majority would not respect the republican principle of freedom of conscience as an inalienable right. The basic inalienable right to religious liberty must be maintained lest all our precious rights become insecure. If the Virginia legislature were permitted to exercise this power, the legislature might not stop with this violation. Indeed, unless checked, the legislature might transform itself into "an independent and hereditary assembly." Hence resist the beginning, and by the defeat of a general religious assessment, extinguish "forever the ambitious hope of making laws for the human mind."[7]

It was important, Madison held, "to take alarm at the first experiment on our liberties" and to act accordingly. Such had been the response of America's Revolutionary Fathers. Such "prudent jealousy" was the "first duty of citizens, and one of [the] noblest characteristics of the late Revolution. The freemen of America did not wait till usurped power had strengthened itself by exercise, and entangled the question in precedents. They saw all the consequences in the principle, and they avoided the consequences by denying the principle."[8]

In brief, analysis required that one anticipate and defeat the anti-republican danger by forceful republican action. Sometimes, however, this was easier said than done. Two famous passages from *The Federalist* illustrate what Madison said to anticipate the future danger of abuse of power by the central government, a danger he was, frankly, not worried about in 1787 and 1788. But what was to be done did not emerge until the danger became real in the 1790s. "In framing a government which is to be administered by men over men, the great difficulty lies in this: you must first enable the government to control the governed; and in the next place oblige it to control itself." And: "The aim of every political constitution is, or ought to be, first to obtain for rulers men who possess most wisdom to discern, and most virtue to pursue, the common good of the society; and in the next place, to take the most effectual precautions for keeping them virtuous whilst they continue to hold their public trust."[9] But only later, in the 1790s, would Madison see a republican political party—in opposition to the national government—and a free press as vital in criticizing and thus controlling the government, and in keeping public officials virtuous.

A further example of Madison's anticipation of the antirepublican danger can be seen in his advocacy of a Bill of Rights in the first session of the new Congress. Earlier, prior to the adoption of the Constitution, Madison, it is true, had been reluctant to include in it a Bill of Rights. He dragged his feet on this matter, oddly, because he felt that the inclusion of a Bill of Rights would limit the protection afforded to liberty, and thus jeopardize the adoption of the Constitution. He feared that a specification of rights might limit the freedoms enjoyed by Americans. Some might argue that the rights to be enjoyed were to be limited to those specified in the Constitution and were thus not to include the broader range of rights included in the state constitutions and reserved to the people. He felt that the basic freedoms would be adequately protected by bills of rights in the state constitutions. Moreover, such freedoms were needed primarily against state government rather than against the central government, which was not, for Madison in 1787, the primary enemy of individual rights. And, in any event, he held that these freedoms could not really be protected against factional majorities in the states if they really wanted to abuse their powers. Besides, to postpone the adoption of the Constitution until a Bill of Rights was included might open the way to renewed discord and anarchy.[10]

Although still not yet alarmed by the danger of violation of rights at the beginning of the first Congress, under the Constitution of 1787, Madison nevertheless took the initiative in introducing a Bill of Rights. His remarks make clear his consistent devotion to republican rights, rights which he deemed crucial for the maintenance of republican government. Indeed, his original proposals constitute a more far-reaching protection for individual rights than that provided in the final Bill of Rights adopted. At this time Madison would have guarded certain rights against both the central government and the various state governments. Here he anticipated both the Civil War amendments (as they protected certain individual rights against state violation) and the twentieth century Supreme Court decisions, by which the Court has read into the meaning of liberty in the Fourteenth Amendment the basic rights of the Bill of Rights.[11]

The basic point in Madison's analysis can now be briefly summarized: in the interest of the maintenance of republican politics, place certain basic rights—e.g., freedom of religion, freedom of speech and press—beyond the reach of governmental power, federal or state.

I have taken so long to get to the fuller development of Madison's theory of democratic politics in the 1790s because I think it is important to demonstrate that not all the ingredients of that theory were fashioned anew in the 1790s. Clearly, even before he was required to focus on the anti-republican danger in the Federalist program, a number of points in his analysis had emerged: establish and maintain a strong and alert republican government to prevent anti-republican "intrusions"; boldly sound the alarm at the first experiment on republican liberties; energetically act to strengthen republican government, and rest assured that vigorous leadership is justified by the principle of republican self-preservation and popular approbation; do not hesitate to resist the beginning of tyranny; see the anti-republican consequences in the heretical principle and avoid the consequences by denying the principle; learn how to control government and to keep public officials virtuous; place certain basic freedoms beyond the reach of governmental power.

With this background in mind, we can now elaborate on Madison's theory of democratic politics as it developed in the 1790s, and then as it received a final formulation in his mind in the 1820s and 1830s.

Before the adoption of the Constitution, Madison had sought to minimize the effects of the reaction against republican government by establishing a more nearly perfect republican union. In the 1790s he had to contend with the worst possible threat to republican union. This was the execution of a factional program at the national level by what he deemed an anti-republican party. What was his analysis of this party and this danger?

That party arose, Madison wrote in 1792, with the "regular and effectual establishment of the federal government in 1788." It consisted of "those, who ... are more partial to the opulent than to the other classes of society; and having debauched themselves into a persuasion that mankind are incapable of governing themselves, it follows with them ... that government can be carried on only by the pageantry of rank, the influence of money and emoluments, and the terror of military force." Indeed, the anti-republican party believed that to the "stupid, suspicious, licentious" people one should pronounce "but two words—*Submission* and *Confidence*."[12]

Throughout Madison's arguments against such measures and actions as the funding of the debt, the bank bill, Washington's neutrality proclamation as defended by Hamilton, Adams' supposed "monarchical principles" and "heretical politics," and the Alien and Sedition Acts, there runs the common threat of the danger to republicanism. Madison feared, perhaps unduly, the corruption of the public interest to the advantage of special interests, the conversion of a limited government into an unlimited one, the obliteration of basic civil liberties, the consolidation of the states into one sovereignty, the undue extension of presidential power, and eventually the transformation of "the present republican system of the United States into an absolute, or, at best, a mixed monarchy."[13]

As Madison analyzed the theory and practice of the Federalist party, he became convinced that to allow an expansive interpretation of federal power by anti-republican forces to go unchallenged was to court suicide. His earlier parade of horribles, mobilized against such measures as the first bank bill, might have been discounted as partisan exaggeration; but the anti-republican danger manifest in the Alien and Sedition Acts was now clear for all to see. The Sedition Act, in particular, was a dramatic illustration of "a power which, more than any other, ought to produce universal alarm, because it is levelled against the rights of freely examining public characters and measures, and of free communication among the people thereon, which has ever been justly deemed the only effectual guardian of every other right."[14]

This was strong language! Here one clearly sees Madison's disposition to "write large" the consequences of deviation from true republican principles. Here, too, objective analysis and partisan protest overlapped. However, if strong partisan exaggeration characterized Madison's analysis of the Federalist party as "anti-republican," it was because he was convinced that such language was necessary to identify the character of the extreme Federalists and to maintain the pure republican faith. He sought, moreover, to maintain this faith in a sometimes hysterical environment marked by such events as the Whiskey Rebellion and the widespread adverse reaction to the French Revolution and its agents. Madison was no uncritical admirer of the French Revolution and everything done in its name. But he did want to prevent the reaction to the French Revolution, and to such fools as the French Minister Plenipotentiary to the United States, Citizen Genêt, from becoming a reaction against republicanism in general. Madison was aware of the fact that the Federalists sought to identify the American Republicans with the French Jacobins and, with the help of the opprobrium heaped upon both, to discredit the Republican party. This he sought to avoid in his sharp counter-attack.[15]

Later in his life, after he had retired from the presidency, and when the "Republican Ascendency" seemed assured, Madison again went forth to battle against the anti-republican forces. This time he was battling against the anti-republican principles inherent in the ideology of nullification and secession. Here Madison cannot be accused of partisan exaggeration. Nonetheless, his characteristic tendency to "write large" anti-republican principles, designs, and actions is again unmistakable. Those who held majority government to be the most oppressive of all governments he believed to be anti-republican. Such a "doctrine strikes at the roots of Republicanism, and if pursued into its consequences, must terminate in absolute monarchy, with a standing military force...." Those who hold such a doctrine in order to attack the tariff "must either join the avowed disciples of aristocracy, oligarchy, or monarchy, or look for" a utopian society.[16]

141

Madison perceived that Calhoun's politics, grounded as it was in a rejection of rule by the numerical majority, was really the politics of anarchy or the politics of tyranny. Calhoun wanted to have his cake and eat it, too. He wanted to protect slavery and the South's other economic and social interests within the Union, but he was unwilling to extend the power to nullify and secede to geographical, political, or economic interests within a given state. In rejecting majority rule Calhoun was rejecting democratic politics; and he must therefore opt either for non-republican government or for anarchy. Nullification and secession were clearly republican heresies and they would destroy not only republican government but the Union as well.

Political Debate and Popular or Party Protest.   As we have seen, analysis of the anti-republican danger cannot be separated from political debate or from popular and party protest. Moreover, debate and protest are themselves intimately linked. Sometimes the political debate would follow the popular protest; sometimes the popular protest would support or follow the political argument. Here, as we move to develop these points in Madison's theory of democratic politics, we need only note the following. First, popular protest was an old revolutionary strategy, but Madison's emphasis on the crucial role of a free press and an informed public opinion would, in the 1790s, give his statement a very modern ring. Second, the organization of a political party with intent to take over the government by peaceful and constitutional means was, in part, novel, and certainly of great significance for the evolution of democratic government.

Earlier in his political career, in the "Memorial and Remonstrance Against Religious Assessments" (1785), Madison had utilized successfully the technique of strong popular protest to rally first a popular and then a legislative majority against the actions threatening republican liberties in Virginia. He had also made effective use of his essays in *The Federalist* and had argued persuasively in the Virginia Ratifying Convention to secure a public opinion favorable to the new constitution. Already then, before the 1790s, he was an old hand at mobilizing support for republican purposes. Now he proceeded to put these talents to work against key portions of the Federalist program.

In a republic, public opinion was crucial because it could ultimately overturn men and policies unable to command the support of a majority of the electorate. Public opinion was a mighty force in the affairs of state. Even the British government, Madison noted, was "maintained less by the distribution of its powers than by the force of public opinion."[17]

Of course, the right leadership was highly essential in keeping the people well-informed and alert. "If an early and well-digested effort for calling out the real sense of the people be not made, there is room to apprehend they may in many places be misled.... We shall endeavor at some means of repelling the danger; particularly by setting on foot expressions of the public mind in important Counties, and under the auspices of respectable names."[18]

It was particularly necessary to combat the Sedition Act because it threatened to deprive republican critics of government of the right to examine public men and measures—and, therefore, of the power to ensure that control and virtue which Madison in *The Federalist* had insisted was essential to good government.

It would seem that the Federalist program caused Madison to place more reliance upon the people than he had previously. In the 1790s the more popularly-democratic Madison emerged in response to political realities which dictated reliance upon the people as a way of defeating the Federalists. Earlier, Madison had been unsure of the popular forces arrayed on the side of the anti-Federalists. Yet he still took his case before the bar of public opinion. In both instances—in 1787 and 1788, and in the 1790s—republican leadership and eventual popular approval were the bases of his theory.

A free press was, Madison argued, essential to enlighten public opinion in an extensive republic. If the republic was too extensive, it might be extremely difficult, if not impossible, to enlighten the people and expect them to overcome faction in actual control of the central government. Here, in a sense, Madison had to argue against his own theory of the difficulty of concert in an extensive republic. Here he had to show that a free press, operating throughout the widespread American republic, could indeed enlighten public opinion against an anti-republican faction whose command of the central government was made more secure by the size of the country. Here, then, Madison was required to add to his theory of the extensive republic. A too extensive republic, he conceded, might be unfavorable to liberty, if—for example—such size called for a powerful central government to maintain order and did not permit its overthrow if it became tyrannical. This would be the case, Madison recognized, unless a free press and other devices which *facilitate* "a general intercourse of sentiments" could enlighten public opinion and thus enable the people to "set bounds" to free government. If the press did not do this, it would be influenced by government; it would become the tool of tyranny instead of tyranny's foe.[19]

However, a knowledgeable, well-organized, and determined republican political party must assist both the press and public opinion in fighting against the anti-republican danger throughout the nation and within governmental circles. Such a party would be indispensable both in rallying the public against the Federalists and in fighting them within the structure of the central government. This party must have broad popular support. Its political slogan must be the public interest. Its chief political argument would be strict constitutional construction.

Thus, by the 1790s, the exigencies of politics had made Madison see the vital importance of parties—not only to govern but also to oppose. However, even though, in the early 1790s, Madison as a practical politician had come to see the necessity of a Republican party to oppose the Federalist party, he still was unable to distinguish clearly between interests and parties. He still found it difficult to escape the conclusion that parties, if unavoidable, were nevertheless evil. Under the political duress of being in the minority in the central government, Madison had recognized the need for a loyal opposition party. However, because of certain aspects of its program, he was reluctant to concede that the governing Federalist party might be a legitimate governing party. He was, then, at this time still groping his way toward a modern theory of politics. That he did not at this time state the modern theory of parties is all the more intriguing because it is implicit in the idea so central to his theory of the extensive republic, the idea of liberty emerging from the competition of contending interests. Unfortunately, party was still too closely associated with interest and faction to be considered legitimate and a necessary and desirable feature of republican government. Only later in his life, as the party system itself developed, did Madison become more aware of the creative role parties could play. Then he saw more clearly the role of parties both in contesting anti-republican faction and in holding the Union together against divisive sectional forces.[20]

Madison, of course, did not limit himself to strict constitutional construction of such key constitutional clauses as the "necessary and proper" and the "general welfare" clauses—a construction which has been examined in an earlier chapter. For example, in protesting against the Alien and Sedition Acts, his attack virtually ran the gamut of constitutional argument. The Acts, he said, represented an exercise of power not delegated. They contravened explicit prohibitions of the federal Bill of Rights. They violated the principle of separation of powers. They would "inflict a deathwound on the sovereignty of the States." They subverted the "general principles of free government." They were not authorized by a Constitution which (the Federalists erroneously contended) embodied common law by implication. They could not be sanctioned by the Preamble to the Constitution. They were not a legitimate exercise of "preventive justice." They were not justified by any governmentally inherent power of self-preservation. They stifled liberty under the guise of controlling the licentiousness of the press. They could be used to justify domestic tyranny under the pretext of combating foreign danger.[21]

The objective of Madison's attack on the wisdom and constitutionality of such legislation as the Alien and Sedition Acts, the first bank bill, and other special-interest legislation, remained the preservation of a Republican Federal Union, including above all the vital republican rights of free speech, free press, free communication, and free elections. Without these rights an opposition republican party could not function; without these rights the Republic would not long endure.

145

In the heat of the partisan battle with the Federalists, Madison sometimes found it difficult to remain a balanced and responsible statesman. Yet his sometimes exaggerated response should not obscure his fundamental contribution in this battle—his contribution to a theory of republican opposition. Madison's theory of opposition deserves much more attention than it has received. Most students of political science, and of democratic politics, now consider the role of the opposing party to be as important for democratic politics as the role of the governing party. Madison helped to develop in America the concept of such a party. His party would oppose in what we today call a loyal, peaceful, and constitutional way. Although Madison attacked both the wisdom and the constitutionality of certain Federalist measures, his use of constitutional argument helped greatly to establish the idea of peaceful constitutional change. Such change must be in accord with basic republican principles. It must be based on public opinion functioning through constitutional machinery. It must be peaceful republican change, and must rest upon the rights of freedom of speech, press, and communication.

Because Madison's Virginia Resolutions have acquired an unsavory aura as a result of their association with Calhoun's concept of nullification, we have sometimes failed to appreciate Madison's contribution to a theory of a loyal, republican opposition. Part of the difficulty, here, is his. The very ambiguity and unorthodoxy of his extreme political remedy of the majority, ultraconstitutional interposition, have led some to question his commitment to a genuinely loyal republican opposition. Both the orthodox and unorthodox character of his theory of political opposition will be examined. Now it is only necessary to emphasize that both his unorthodox ideas and his tortured construction of key constitutional clauses illustrate the lengths to which this sober-minded, scholarly student of political life would go to protest against the anti-republican danger and to guard crucial civil rights against attack. In the "Memorial and Remonstrance," he had stressed the necessity of denying anti-republican principles to avoid anti-republican consequences. Now that the anti-republican consequences were dangerously evident (particularly in the Sedition Act), he did not flinch from constitutional interpretation, however strained, to counter such consequences. Madison, we must remember, did not take the plunge into nullification. And, later in his life, he used his defense of his position in the Virginia Resolutions as a scalpel to dissect and excise the doctrine of nullification and secession. Consistently, he held that the republican opposition must still remain loyal to those principles of majority rule and aggregate popular sovereignty without which republican government could not endure. Madison's theory of a loyal republican opposition will become clearer as we turn now to examine both the orthodox and unorthodox ideas he advocated for democratic politics.

Orthodox Constitutional Means. Madison hoped that argument based on the merits and constitutionality of a given measure might kill such anti-republican measures before passage. If such argument failed, however, he was prepared to fight against such measures after passage. Despite what may seem a suggestive flirtation with a less respectable doctrine, he held that public opinion—if enlightened with the aid of state initiative—would respond to such anti-republican measures by using legitimate techniques of electoral opposition. State legislatures could petition Congress for repeal of obnoxious and unconstitutional measures. They could also request the state's own congressmen to propose constitutional amendments. A sufficient number of state legislatures could petition Congress to propose amendments to the Constitution. A President could be impeached for violating his trust. And as public opinion could result in a legislative change of mind, it could also lead to a judicial change of mind.[22]

Hence, the Virginia Resolutions could mean simply those techniques of opposition which are quite orthodox by today's standards. Superficially, the Virginia Resolutions asked the other states to concur with Virginia in declaring the Alien and Sedition Acts unconstitutional. This could be simply a declaration of opinion. The Resolutions called for "interposition" and for "necessary and proper measures" by other states "for cooperating" with Virginia in "maintaining unimpaired the authorities, rights, and liberties reserved to the States respectively, or the people." This could be a request for the employment of the usual constitutional methods for the redress of grievances.[23]

In appraising Madison's ideas on this subject, we must not forget that some of his opponents denied that a state might protest against the constitutionality of federal legislation. They also denied the propriety of appealing a constitutional question beyond the federal judiciary.[24] In view of these denials, Madison's defense of the freedom of the states—and the people in the states—to communicate ideas challenging the constitutionality of federal legislation and to take the initiative in seeking change via appeal, elections, and amendment, becomes not a commonplace defense of the obvious but a vindication of republican principles under challenge.

This, at least, is the way Madison saw it. One can never know precisely what he would have done if the Alien and Sedition Acts had remained in force under an extremist Federalist administration. Historically, we know that the Virginia Resolutions have been subject to interpretations different from Madison's, interpretations full of mischief for the more nearly perfect republican union.

Ultraconstitutional Interposition. Madison contended, however, that these (now orthodox) means did not exhaust the possibilities open to the sovereign people of the states, as parties to and creators of the Constitution, who could, therefore, explain, amend, and remake the Constitution. He maintained that ultraconstitutional interposition remained as a penultimate resort in "those great and extraordinary cases in which all the forms of the Constitution may prove ineffectual against infractions dangerous to the essential rights of the parties to it." The exact nature of this ultraconstitutional remedy—this extreme remedy to be employed only in rare cases—remains somewhat mysterious. Madison never spelled out its exact nature. He did indicate that such a remedy must secure a peaceful and effective decision. It cannot be employed when the oppressed are a minority and the oppressors a majority. In other words, there is no ultimate, constitutional power on the part of a minority to explain, amend, or remake a constitution. Apparently, only a majority (presumably a majority of people in a majority of states) possesses this ultimate, constitutional power as the parties to and creators of the Constitution. So long as the minority stays within the Union and under the Union's Constitution, not even its desperate, oppressed position enables it to invoke Madison's doctrine of ultraconstitutional interposition.[25]

Later, in the midst of the nullification controversy, Madison insisted strongly that the interposition called for by the Virginia Resolutions would not justify South Carolina's nullification of federal legislation. He denied, too, South Carolina's claim that such single-state nullification was valid until overridden by three-fourths of the other states in the Union. Rather, he maintained, interposition called for the collective, aggregate, concurrent action of the sovereign people of the states. Furthermore, the Virginia Resolutions constituted a declaration of opinion only. They were not self-executing. The extreme remedy of ultraconstitutional interposition involved only the exercise of an ultimate constitutional power inherent in a free people. The Resolutions did not invoke a natural right of revolution to be employed by protesting forces while they remained within the existing constitutional order.[26]

The Appeal to Revolution. Madison was a strong believer in constitutional government and in constitutional resistance to anti-republican measures. But, in his theory of democratic politics, he never abandoned that republican orientation which justified revolution—armed revolt, if necessary—as the *ultimate* remedy by a majority or a minority against intolerable oppression. In taking this stand, he was simply endorsing an orthodox philosophy immortalized by his close friend, Jefferson, in the Declaration of Independence. Madison clearly recognized that the remedy of revolution was a natural (or moral) right and not a constitutional (or legal) right. It was a natural right because "intolerable oppression" of the people by government, and "abuse or usurpations" by government, released the sovereign people in the states from their obligations under the Constitution. They were, however, not isolated individuals back in a state of nature. Rather they remained in society but outside the jurisdiction of the government which had violated their trust embodied in the constitutional compact. As far as the intolerably oppressed were concerned, government was dissolved. The parties to the constitutional compact might, therefore, use their "natural right of self-preservation" to revolt against governmental tyranny and set up a new government which would again embody the people's trust and hence command their constitutional obedience. Madison later conceded that nullification was such a natural right.[27]

However, even though Madison conceded to an intolerably oppressed majority or minority a natural (or moral) right to revolt, he did not issue an impetuous call to revolt. Even under conditions of intolerable oppression, he felt, one must carefully weigh the consequences of resistance and oppression. Should "power usurped be sustained in its oppressive exercise by a majority, the final course to be pursued by the minority must be a subject of calculation, in which the degrees of oppression, the means of resistance, the consequences of its failure, and the consequences of its success must be the elements."[28]

III

I have tried in the preceding section to develop the major ingredients of Madison's theory of democratic politics. This theory, I have suggested, emerged more fully in response to the question of how to cope with the anti-republican danger. Democratic politics, Madison insisted, rested upon the protection of basic civil liberties, particularly freedom of speech, press, assembly. Democratic politics demanded an alert and informed public opinion, a free press, and a vigorous republican opposition to ensure the election and control of virtuous public officials. Vigorous republican leadership was essential to ensure that protection and also the maintenance of a sound and more uniform republican policy throughout the nation. Such leadership, relying upon strict constitutional interpretation, would peacefully oppose anti-republican measures through the instrumentality of a republican party opposition. These were the main ideas.

In developing these ideas Madison may have pushed strict constitutional interpretation too far, but push it he did, with the consequent development of constitution worship in the United States. Retrospectively, many critics may question strict constitutional construction, but few can deny that Madison committed the Republican party to constitutional opposition. The ambiguity of that opposition as it became ultraconstitutional interposition has obscured somewhat its constitutional character. And, therefore, a few further words are in order. This further clarification calls attention to the fact that Madison in the Virginia Resolutions and in the "Notes on Nullification" was really exploring at the uncertain border of democratic politics, particularly as democratic theoreticians are required to face up to the problem of republican opposition.

Candidly, it is no easy matter to nail down the precise meaning of the Virginia Resolutions even in the light shed by his later "Notes on Nullification."[29] Madison's main purpose in the "Notes" is clear enough: he wanted to distinguish his own theory of republican opposition from that of the advocates of nullification and secession. And he does so. His was constitutional; theirs was not. Yet he is not successful in clarifying beyond dispute the meaning of ultraconstitutional interposition. How does this term really differ from the natural right of revolution, of which nullification is an example?

Both were ultimate resorts for Madison. They were ultimate, first, because a "revolt" against the accepted legal order was involved and, second, because the existing constitutional machinery would not be employed. However, if my interpretation is correct, ultraconstitutional interposition was a doctrine that could be invoked only by a majority, more accurately by a majority of people in a majority of states, and might *peacefully* alter or reform a given constitution. Such "revolt" was not legal since it constituted an appeal to the people over the heads of the existing legal government and its legal machinery. This view might perhaps be called the ultimate, peaceful, constituent power of a majority in a republic. An illustration of such interposition might be the position taken by the rebels in Dorr's Rebellion in Rhode Island in 1842. This, by the way, was the losing position in *Luther v. Borden* (1849). A popular majority in the state was not allowed to bypass the existing constitutional machinery in order to secure constitutional reform.

Nonpeaceful revolution by a minority—the invocation of the natural right of revolution—was still another alternative in defense of basic rights against oppression. Such action could not be truly constituent because it was not based on the majority. Presumably, in a genuinely *republican* society there would be no need for nonpeaceful revolution by a majority because those in the majority could employ the constitutional machinery to secure what they wanted. (This questionable premise will be returned to in a moment.) However, Madison recognized, nonpeaceful revolution might still have to be invoked in extreme cases. It was based on a natural or moral right to revolt. It was a "revolt" that would not only overthrow the existing government and obnoxious laws but could theoretically put a minority of the righteous in power until such time as this minority could convince the obstinate majority to go along with its rightful republican position. The clearcut assumption in Madison and in other Republican thinkers was that a majority would ultimately support such revolt. Nullification by a minority in the South would not lead to these results!

But what would happen if the majority in a republic was unable to use the constitutional machinery peacefully—either the normal machinery or the ultimate constituent power of the people to overturn a tyrannical and anti-republican minority in command of the government? Might not majoritarian ultraconstitutional interposition have to terminate in an armed revolt if the government in power refused to surrender peacefully to the majoritarian rebels?

This important question was never satisfactorily answered by Madison. In the battle against the Alien and Sedition Acts he had enunciated a doctrine of opposition designed to step up the pressure against an unpopular government and its unpopular measures. He did not then appreciate that the ambiguity of his doctrine might indeed be interpreted in other ways. Moreover, the doctrine, as perverted, might become a poison tip of the arrow of state sovereignty and mortally wound the Union.

Of course, Madison did deny that nullification was a constitutional right, or an example of ultraconstitutional interposition. For him it was an exercise—foolish, ill-advised, dangerous—of the natural right to revolt. He also pointed out that the advocates of nullification had lost sight of the important distinctions among a *usurpation,* an *abuse*, and an *unwise use* of power. These distinctions are a healthy emphasis in any theory of democratic politics, as this calls for prudence in the political opposition. (1) A *usurpation* was an *unconstitutional* action taken *without the support of the popular majority.* Here government assumed unwarranted power in opposition to the will of the majority of the people. In this case, "nothing is necessary but to rouse the attention of the people, and a remedy ensues thro' the forms of the Constitution. This was seen when the Constitution was violated by the Alien and Sedition Acts." (2) An *abuse* was an *unconstitutional* action taken *with the support of the popular majority.* It was unwarranted but based on popular consent. Federal expenditures for roads and canals, without a constitutional amendment authorizing such expenditures, illustrated such an abuse. In this case, "the appeal can only be made to the recollections, the reason, and the conciliatory spirit of the majority of the people against their own errors; with a persevering hope of success, and an eventual acquiescence in disappointment unless indeed oppression should reach an extremity overruling all other considerations." (3) Finally, Madison pointed out, there could also be an *unwise use* of constitutional power. A clear example here was a discriminatory or onerous tariff. Here, too, the measure *might have popular support.*[30]

Each of these exercises of power called for a different kind of opposition, a different political response. For example, there could be no compromise with the Alien and Sedition Acts; they must be made inoperative. Internal improvements were wise, if unconstitutional; hence a constitutional amendment or prescriptive usage would give them validity. A discriminatory tariff was constitutional, if unwise; here political statesmanship was needed. Unless the advocates of nullification appreciated the differences among usurpation, abuse, and unwise use of power, Madison maintained, they would jeopardize republican union. Nullification—an illustration of the natural (or moral) right to revolt—was not the appropriate response for an unwise use of constitutional power. Only continued usurpation could justify ultraconstitutional interposition *if* the regular constitutional machinery was unavailing. Even in this case, the right of revolution was the ultimate resort outside the constitutional framework.[31]

IV

Finally, how does one appraise Madison's theory of democratic politics that emerged as a response to the anti-republican danger in America? Initially, it should be clear that his theory of democratic politics—as it embraces notions of civil liberties, bold leadership, and republican political opposition—lacks systematic statement. This is truer here than it is with regard to his strong nationalism as an appropriate response to disunion, his defense of federalism as a "middle-ground" remedy for the problem of large size, or his advocacy of the extensive republic as an explanation of how faction could be controlled. His theory of democratic politics must be pieced together with considerable intellectual hazard. There is a rough pattern, I have suggested, but it is not a finished pattern. However, despite the incomplete pattern, a sense of democratic politics does emerge. If put into aphoristic imperatives, the theory would appear as follows:

—Safeguard the basic civil liberties, for without freedom of speech and press and assembly, there can be no free elections, no criticism of public officials, no republican policy.

—Be prepared to exert bold leadership in anticipation of the anti-republican danger.

—Know your friends and foes; take alarm at the selfish friends and scheming foes, and be prepared to organize a genuinely republican party to advance truly republican principles.

—Resist the beginning of trouble and tyranny—by protesting loudly and intensely.

—See the untoward consequences in the wrong principles —and thus avoid the consequences by denying the principles.

—Be careful to distinguish among a usurpation, an abuse, and an unwise use of power.

—Use orthodox constitutional interpretation and constitutional weapons first, but do not abandon peaceful, majoritarian recourse to the people—the highest source of constituent power—if such recourse beyond the existing legal order is necessary.

—Always keep in reserve the natural right of militant revolt—in the event that tyranny is continued by a majority against an entrenched minority.

The stress on civil liberties in Madison's theory of democratic politics is remarkably fresh today. Madison emerges as an early spokesman for the American tradition of civil liberties which emphasizes the greater freedom needed by republican citizens to criticize public men and measures. Madison stands in the front rank of those battling to establish American libertarian concepts of civil rights. Indeed, he might even be called the father of the doctrine of preferred freedoms.

His theory of bold leadership calls attention to another modern political idea: the need to anticipate difficulties and not simply react to them. Here Madison, frankly, was not uniformly successful. He anticipated a broader conception of religious liberty in 1785, a stronger concept of federal union in 1787, and a more far-reaching Bill of Rights in 1791; but he did not successfully anticipate the threats inherent in key Federalist policies until they were thrust upon him. Then, perhaps with the exception of his response to the Sedition Act, he overreacted. He was, however, at the end of his life able to anticipate the disaster of the Civil War; but at this time he lacked the political power to head off this catastrophe.

He was able, however, to develop an embryonic theory of republican political opposition—based firmly upon civil liberties, bold leadership, a free press, an alert and informed public opinion, a loyal constitutional opposition, and the indispensability of parties to the maintenance of freedom. He used this theory to clarify the anti-republican character of both the Alien and Sedition Acts and the doctrines of nullification and secession, all of which he saw as hostile to a theory of democratic politics. If unchallenged, the former acts would be fatal to republican freedom, the latter to both republicanism and union. The extreme remedy he played around with, the doctrine of ultraconstitutional interposition, calls attention to the difficulties inherent in any theory of opposition. Madison perhaps knew that when a republican society reached the point of invoking extreme remedies, serious troubles loomed ahead. Why? Because then the underlying consensus tying a republican nation together had been destroyed. It may be that Madison refused to spell out the details of ultraconstitutional interposition more clearly because he felt that the potential threat involved here—the appeal to the people over the heads of their existing rulers—would normally be sufficient to induce actual or potential usurpers to correct their ways.

In articulating a theory of democratic politics Madison never lost sight of the need to balance liberty and power, freedom and order. The prudent democratic statesman might have to shift his emphasis from one side to the other of these polar values, but he would never lose sight of the need to achieve a republican balance.

"Being republicans ... [we] must be anxious ... in defending liberty against power, and power against licentiousness."

"Liberty and order will never be *perfectly* safe, until a trespass on the constitutional provisions for either shall be felt with the same keenness that resents an invasion of the dearest rights, until every citizen shall be an ARGUS to espy and an AEGEON to avenge, the unhallowed deed."[32]

This prudential balancing of liberty and power, freedom and order must, indeed, be the central endeavor of a modern theory of democratic politics.

CHAPTER 7

Madison and Democracy
in America

> *"Is it not the glory of the people of America, that, whilst they have paid a decent regard to the opinions of former times and other nations, they have not suffered a blind veneration for antiquity, for customs, or for names, to overrule the suggestions of their own good sense, the knowledge of their own situation, and the lessons of their own experience? To this manly spirit, posterity will be indebted for the possession and the world for the example, of the numerous innovations displayed on the American theatre, in favor of private rights and public happiness."*
> — *The Federalist,* Number 14

In conclusion, it may be helpful to match Madison's political theory against an outline of modern democratic theory in order to see Madison's relevance to our present discontents.[1] This contrast may throw considerable light on the validity, viability, and significance of Madison's political theory.

The risks of such an endeavor are great. One may succeed in attributing to Madison a comprehensiveness, a modernity, a sharpness, and a foresight that are nowhere to be found in his thought. However, such a comparison may highlight the failings, shortcomings, and weaknesses of Madison's theory as well as its successes, merits, and strengths. Such a juxtaposition may enable the appraiser either to cut an alleged hero down to size or to puff up a second-rater until he appears as a neglected superman. Keeping constantly in mind that such matching may be only as valuable as the model which provides the basis for comparison, one can attempt to relate

157

Madison's theory to a modern democratic model. In this way one can note more pointedly Madison's contribution to democratic theory today.

James Madison was by no means a systematic, comprehensive, sophisticated student of political theory. He never undertook to set forth his political philosophy as might a professional philosopher. He did not critically examine or reexamine his basic philosophic premises. He made no conscious effort to fit the pieces of his political theory together in a well-articulated whole. Yet notwithstanding these undeniable facts, one can find in Madison's thought the germ of a durable, penetrating, and persuasive democratic theory for man today.

Thus Madison did not talk about the normative, empirical, and prudential *components of political theory,* the components that are concerned, respectively, with what ought to be, with what is, and with what can be. Nor was he very sophisticated about the intimate relationship of these three elements. Yet he had a very clear appreciation of the primacy of the normative factors involved in his republican ideology. He had a keen understanding of the reality of such empirical considerations as the behavior of men, interests, and states as they struggled for power. And he was astute in recognizing the importance of a prudential guide to assure the establishment and maintenance of republicanism in the New World. Indeed, his entire political theory was dominated by the recognition that a republican guide to action can be worked out only in the light of political realities. Implicit in this outlook was a thorough awareness that political theory involves the harmonious reconciliation of humankind's goals and the hard facts of political life in a successful program of public policy.

Nowhere in his published writings did Madison enunciate and justify in systematic fashion the basic value-judgments of his political theory. Yet if he did not clearly state and defend what some modern democratic theorists would agree is the *primary value-judgment* of modern democratic theory—self-realization within the framework of the common good—it is clear that he believed that liberty, justice, safety, and happiness in society were essential to the achievement of self-realization. In seeking such realization one should not be unmindful of the legitimate role of authority or the persistent claims of the community. The realization involved was optimum realization, the freest and fullest possible realization compatible with the common good. This meant only the realization of man's unique, good, and creative potentialities. This concept of realization was grounded in a conscious commitment to liberty and diversity in the faculties of men. It was also based on the sober, if obvious, conclusion that absolute freedom and fulfillment were impossible. It was confirmed by the inevitable and unhappy presence of evil and destructive potentialities in men which must be brought under control lest the public good be sacrificed. Madison's republican ideology thus achieved an unquestioned primacy in his theory. This ideology shaped and colored the nature of his entire guide to action. There was little or no epistemological defense of Madison's primary value-judgment in his writings. This judgment was assumed. Madison's concern was the pragmatic one of establishing a government that would safeguard and advance this judgment. It was not the metaphysical concern of settling doubts as to the meaning of the "true" and the "just."

In his political theory Madison also adhered to a concept of *limits*, a theme which has taken a more and more prominent position in modern democratic theory. For Madison, the possibility of human realization was decidedly limited. It is precisely his recognition of a theory of limits which makes him so appealing to some modern political thinkers. These limits, he argued, are inherent in the nature of man and in the world in which he lives. Initially, man must recognize that he is mortal, sinful, fallible, and finite. He is not God. He is neither angel nor philosopher-king. The fulfillment of objectives is restricted by man's ineradicable liberty and diversity. These prevent homogeneity of interests. They make perfect political harmony impossible, and even "normal" harmony difficult. Frequently, men are dominated by passion instead of reason. They are governed by self-interest, not the public good. They are driven by immoral motives of power and self-aggrandizement rather than by a nobler ethics and a disinterested respect for justice. The abuse of power, attested by reason and historical experience, is thus rooted in the very character of man. Consequently, utopian human realization is even theoretically impossible. The acceptance of wise limits, ordained by God and Natural Law, is the beginning of realistic political science.

But if there are upper limits to man's possible and feasible development, there are also, Madison maintained, lower limits to his decline which are reinforced by man's *intelligence and will.* The keen recognition of the mortality of all governments, including republican governments, is a constant challenge to man's intelligence and his responsible action. When these combine, one can more easily guard against the plunge into Hell and more safely probe the possibilities of limited but realistic republican advance. For example, the alleged impossibility of republican government in a geographically huge country such as the United States can be offset by a theory such as that of the extensive republic. Men adhering to such a theory can counter the evil effects of not only huge size, but also disunion, faction, and anti-republicanism. In brief, republican realization can be advanced, given the application of republican intelligence and will. And such bold effort holds out the exciting promise of republican fulfillment within wisely ordained limits. Hence, republican theory can appreciate the dangers of utopian progress and perfectibility, while yet permitting—nay, enjoining—progressive fulfillment this side of the sin of pride. Here republican theory paradoxically combines a dynamic view of effort with a sobering view of man's limitations.

With regard to yet another basic concept of modern democratic theory, that of *accommodation,* Madison is still refreshingly relevant. Consciously committed to liberty and human realization, Madison was also consciously aware of the inevitable conflicts stemming from such a commitment. He squarely faced the key questions of republican accommodation. How is it possible—in a way compatible with the republican commitment to life, liberty, property, limits, and effort—to reconcile the inevitable conflicts in republican society? Conflicts between the central government and the self-governing states? Between majorities and minorities? Between groups and individuals? Between the varying economic, social, and political interests that one encounters in a free society? Madison's answer was one that built upon traditional republican theory in an original and creative way. The protection of civil liberties was crucial. Freedom of speech, press, assembly, and elections was primary. Given these, one can achieve accommodation by means of republican and constitutional majority rule as this operates in the extensive republic. The extensive republic was a representative, federal republic embracing a large geographical area and a plurality of interests. In such a republic the multiplicity, diversity, and competition of interests, by diminishing the possibility of factional agreement and unified factional action, increased the ability of a republican government armed with requisite powers to regulate such clashing forces in the public interest. Ultimately, the success of such a republican government rested upon a virtuous people who agreed upon enough fundamentals at any given time to inspire the indispensable consensus of any free, orderly, and civilized society. By such rule in such a republic, conflicts between center and circumference, between majorities and minorities, between groups and individuals, between conflicting interests might be creatively compromised. An emotional and rational trust in the system and in those who operated the system made such creative compromise possible. Minority factions would be controlled by strong, wise, and reasonable majorities, ever conscious of their fluid, ever-changing, and overlapping composition. Majority factions would not have the easy opportunity or the monolithic power, if they had the will, to perpetuate their mischief. A republican party system, operative throughout the union, ever responsive to politically potent minorities, and always concerned with forging a victorious coalition out of frequently diverse and conflicting political forces, would hearken to the intense feelings of adversely affected interests, resist the demands of the extremists, and insist upon compromise of the most seriously divisive issues. A partly federal, partly national concept of union would provide supremacy for the central government, safeguard the appropriate powers of self-government in the states, and assure the individual citizen of his necessary rights. Much of this view of accommodation is still largely valid today. And if Americans can continue to maintain civil liberties, to reinforce consensus at the bottom, the creative role of parties in the middle, and sound governmental leadership at the top, Madison's concept of accommodation becomes even more relevant. Confidence would be placed in an executive-legislative team under the vigorous and resourceful leadership of a President aware of the power and responsibility of his office. Such a President would function as one centrally located, powerfully equipped, and highly significant contender amid the clash of rival interests. He would be able to operate more in accord with the "public interest" because of his broader constituency. He would thus be able more easily to advance positive democratic government in the public interest. He could take the lead in transcending jealous local sovereignties, sectional rivalries, and the inevitable conflicts of interest in a free society and in ensuring the more uniform preservation of private rights and public happiness.

Such a theory of accommodation was also reinforced by a rough concept of *levels of realization.* This concept outlined the respective roles of the individual, the group, and the government in advancing republican realization. Involved here was a large private area for the individual. Above all, the mind of the individual must be free. Involved here, too, was generous room for the innumerable interests of modern society: a church independent of government, a press and an opposition party free to criticize the government in power, independent and self-respecting farmers, merchants, manufacturers, and workers. Division of the public sphere would be ascertained primarily by the necessary, if debatable, concept of due national supremacy. The determination of functions would be strongly guided by the pragmatic principle of approved utility: those organs which can best do a given job will be given the task. The advancement of republican ends—not the dogma of states' rights, or state sovereignty, or private enterprise—would be the deciding principle. And changes in the application of the meaning of due supremacy should not detract from its cardinal importance or the inevitability of new assumptions of power by nation or state as a result of changing circumstances. Shifts in jurisdiction from state to nation or from private groups to government are dictated by prudence, not by some un-American blueprint for remodeling society.

162

However, if change was a law of political life, this did not mean that due supremacy was a meaningless or an ambiguous term. Opposition to the national government at one time might be perfectly consistent with support for it another time. Any theory of accommodation must be dynamic and must recognize changes of policy. However, although difficult to define, there were limits to and principles of *political obligation* which indicated for Madison the line between constitutional accommodation, ultraconstitutional interposition, and militant revolution. Madison argued that the citizen's primary allegiance is to republican principles. When such principles are embodied in a republican federal union, the individual has a constitutional obligation to support such a union. However, constitutional opposition to anti-republican principles is mandatory. The nature and extent of opposition would always have to be influenced by the clarity and imminence of the threat to vital republican principles and the feasibility of accepted legal means of opposition. In the interest of republican self-preservation, the majority might sometimes have to go beyond legal techniques of constitutional opposition, without, however, resorting to armed revolt. Such interposition involved the ultimate constituent power of the sovereign people. It should be employed only in the gravest cases. Theoretically, there was no constitutional right to revolution. There was, however, a moral or natural right to revolt. This right, which could be invoked by a really oppressed minority, would wisely be employed only after a prudent calculation of the ultimate consequences of such action. Madison recognized as desirable a healthy competition among pluralistic groups and levels of government for the loyalty of the republican citizen whose obligation to obey would ultimately spring from his consent. This competition served to protect the citizen's freedom. When the chips were down, however, the citizen's obligation to the most inclusive majority within its rightful sphere, a majority of people in a majority of states as expressed in the constitution and government of the United States, was strong and compelling precisely because it was based on the citizen's consent and operated to advance his realization.

One also finds in Madison's thought a fairly clear expression of the concept of *calculated risk*. This element of democratic theory has been achieving more attention as modern theorists have reappraised the gap between promise and performance in connection with first-class citizenship for Blacks and other disadvantaged minorities in modern America; have realistically reexamined the prospects of successful development among Third World nations; have explored the rivalry among the superpowers and especially probed the dangers of the arms race and nuclear catastrophe; and have analyzed the aspirations of thoughtful women and men for a democratic and constitutional world order. The importance of such a theory of calculated risk is momentous. Such a theory highlights the dangers in democratic theory as a whole, demands a prudent calculation of risks, and requires inevitable reassessment of both calculations and risks in the light of changing circumstances. Madison was aware of the calculated risks inherent in his theory. These risks included the assumption that there was in man a quota of virtue and intelligence sufficient to balance his vice and ignorance. They involved the assumption of a working constitutional order grounded fundamentally in civil liberties, enlightened public opinion, a sound party system, and a minimum consensus among interacting groups in the body politic. They included the possibility of rightful and reasonable majority rule. They incorporated the assumption that the theory of the extensive republic did satisfactorily explain how the effects of faction would be controlled and how, thus, the feasibility of republican government in a large country could be assured. They involved faith in the new operational principles of federalism which were designed to achieve a proper balance between the central government and the state governments. These were a few of the more important risks. To a large extent these risks confront us today. They underscore the importance of regularly recalculating the ideological, operational, and explanatory principles upon which modern democratic theory is based.

Finally, one notes in Madison's theory a recognition of the creative role of political theory and the political theorist. Here one acquires a significant insight into Madison's philosophy of history. He held that America's Promethean spirit can break the oppressive chain of destiny that has hitherto bound republican man to a frightful past. He recognized that political theory builds on past theory and history, and on present experience. He also knew that the political theorist must be creative. His task is pragmatic. He must provide prudent guidance, in the light of political reality, for purposive men. Rightly understood, then, political theory, which has so often been underestimated in the interpretation of American history, can greatly help to make possible a lasting and significant republican adventure in self-realization within the framework of the common good.

Madison does not provide answers to all or even to many of the problems posed by political theorists or plaguing modern man. However, his theory, rightly understood, does embody the spirit, the method, and many of the principles of the true genius of American politics.

This genius America needs again today.

Notes

Chapter 1

1. Irving Brant, "James Madison and His Times," *American Historical Review,* LVII, No. 4 (July, 1952), particularly 854-857.
2. Quoted in Irving Brant, *James Madison: Father of the Constitution, 1787-1800* (Indianapolis: Bobbs-Merrill, 1950), p. 194.
3. See John F. Kennedy, *Profiles in Courage* (1955) (New York: Harper & Row, Memorial Edition, 1964), p. 84.
4. *The Federalist* (1787-1788) (New York: Modern Library, 1937), Number 10, pp. 58-59. Hereinafter, all references will be to this edition of *The Federalist.*
5. Gaillard Hunt, ed., *The Writings of James Madison,* 9 vols. (New York: G. P. Putnam's Sons, 1900-1910). The "let alone" quote is in 9 *Writings* 568 (1835) (To Charles J. Ingersoll). Hereinafter, this is the way I will indicate my reference to volume, page number, and date of quotation from this volume.
6. 6 *Writings* 88 (1792) ("Universal Peace," essay in *The National Gazette).*
7. 9 *Writings* 395 note (1829) (Note during the Convention for Amending the Constitution of Virginia).
8. 5 *Writings* 199 (1788) (Speech in the Virginia Ratifying Convention).
9. 5 *Writings* 49 (1787) (To Archibald Stuart).
10. *Madison's Works: Letters and Other Writings of James Madison,* 4 vols. (New York: R. Worthington, 1884). Published by order of Congress. The quotation is in 1 *Works* 119 (1784) (To Richard H. Lee). Subsequent references will be cited in this way.
11. 5 *Writings* 197 (1788) (Speech in the Virginia Ratifying Convention).
12. 4 *Works* 210 (1831) (To N. P. Trist).
13. 4 *Works* 186 (1831) (To Charles J. Ingersoll).
14. 3 *Works* 483 (1825) (To Thomas Jefferson).

15. 4 *Works* 210 (1831) (To N. P. Trist).
16. The quoted words are Brant's in "James Madison and His Times," p. 868.
17. Charles M. Wiltse, *The Jeffersonian Tradition in American Democracy* (Chapel Hill: University of North Carolina Press, 1935), p. 59.
18. Douglass Adair, ed., "James Madison's Autobiography," *William and Mary Quarterly,* Third Series, II (April, 1945), 195-196.
19. Aristotle's *Politics,* V. 9. 1309^b.
20. *The Federalist,* Number 14, pp. 84-85.

Chapter 2

1. *The Federalist,* Number 39, p. 243.
2. Gaillard Hunt and J. B. Scott, eds.,*The Debates in the Federal Convention of 1787* (New York: Oxford University Press, 1920), pp. 497, 329, 619, note 1. Hereinafter references will be cited simply as *Debates.* The last quoted remark was not made in the Convention. It was a subsequent note made by Madison, amplifying his speech of August 7 on the question of suffrage.
3. *The Federalist,* Number 39, pp. 243-244; and Number 37, p. 227.
4. 9 *Writings* 528 (1833) (Memorandum on "Majority Governments"); 2 *Writings* 366 (1787) ("Vices of the Political System of the United States"); 5 *Writings* 376-377 (1787) (Speech in Congress on Amendments to the Constitution).
5. 5 *Writings* 197 (1788) (Speech in the Virginia Ratifying Convention).
6. *Debates,* pp. 59, 497, and letters to Jefferson (March 18), Randolph (April 8), and Washington (April 16) on the eve of the Convention, 2 *Writings* 326-328, 337-340, 344-349 (1787); *The Federalist,* Number 37, p. 227 and Number 39, pp. 243-244, and also *Debates,* pp. 91, 167-168; *The Federalist,* Number 43, pp. 282-283 and Number 57, p. 371; 2 *Writings* 363 ("Vices . . ."), *Debates,* p. 124, and *The Federalist,* Number 43, pp. 283-284; 5 *Writings* 370-389 (1789) (Speech in Congress on Amendments to the Constitution); 5 *Writings* 359 (1789) (Speech in Congress on Import Duties); 5 *Writings* 355 note (1789) (To Thomas Jefferson); 6 *Writings* 105 (1792) ("The Union: Who Are Its Real Friends?"—essay in *The National Gazette*).
7. 4 *Works* 58 (1830) (To N. P. Trist).

8. See Richard B. Morris' perceptive, well-balanced review of "The Confederation Period and the American Historian," *William and Mary Quarterly,* Third Series, XIII (April, 1956), 139-156.
9. See Aristotle's *Politics,* particularly the conclusion of III, vi, and IV, xi, wherein he treats constitutions and the type of constitution which is most generally practicable.
10. Cicero, *On the Commonwealth,* translated with Notes and Introduction by George H. Sabine and Stanley B. Smith (Columbus: Ohio State University Press, 1929), I, xxv (p. 129); III, xxii (pp. 215-216).
11. For the specific ideas of Machiavelli mentioned in the text, see, for example, *The Prince,* Ch. xxvi, *The Discourses,* Chs. iv, xvii, xxxiv, and lviii. Harrington's appraisal of Machiavelli as "The Only Politician of Later Ages" is found in *The Commonwealth of Oceana* (1656; London: George Routledge and Sons, 1887), p. 17.
12. For these ideas, see Harrington's *Oceana,* pp. 26 and 28. Harrington's famous and influential definition of an "equal commonwealth—incorporating an 'agrarian law,' separation of powers, rotation in office, and a free ballot"—is on p. 40. See particularly Locke's *Second Treatise of Civil Government* and Sydney's *Discourse Concerning Government.*
13. See the modern edition of Althusius' *Politica Methodice Digesta* by C. J. Friedrich (Cambridge, Mass.: Harvard University Press, 1932). For Rousseau on the subject of "confederations," see his promise to treat the problem in *The Social Contract,* III, xv, footnote in the last paragraph. Madison's quoted remark can be found in 6 *Writings* 93 (1792) ("Spirit of Governments," essay in *The National Gazette*).
14. Montesquieu, *The Spirit of Laws,* translated by Thomas Nugent (Cincinnati: Robert Clark, 1873), I, 139, 142, 145-146.
15. Quoted in Douglass Adair, "That Politics May Be Reduced to a Science: David Hume, James Madison, and the Tenth Federalist," *The Huntington Library Quarterly,* XX, No. 4 (August, 1957), 349, 351, 351-353.
16. Ibid., p. 349.
17. Ibid., p. 348.
18. Ibid.
19. Cecelia M. Kenyon, "Men of Little Faith: The Anti-Federalists on the Nature of Representative Government," *William and Mary Quarterly,* Third Series, XII (January, 1956), 6, 38.
20. See particularly 2 *Writings* 367-368 (1787) ("Vices . . ."); *Debates,* pp. 64-65, 167-168; *The Federalist,* Number 10, p. 51; 5

Writings 28-32 (1787) (To Thomas Jefferson); 6 *Writings* 106-119 (1792) ("A Candid State of Parties," essay in *The National Gazette*); 9 *Writings* 361-362 (1829) (Speech in the Virginia Constitutional Convention); 9 *Writings* 520-528 (1833) (Memorandum on "Majority Governments").

21. On faction, see the citations above; on virtue and possibilities of the good republican life, see *Debates,* p. 92; *The Federalist,* Number 14, p. 84, Number 39, p. 243, Number 55, p. 365, Number 57, p. 373, Number 63, pp. 409-410; 5 *Writings* 223 (1788) (Speech in the Virginia Ratifying Convention); 6 *Writings* 120-123 (1792) ("Who Are the Best Keepers of the People's Liberties?"—essay in *The National Gazette*); 6 *Writings* 222 note (1794) (Speech in Congress); 8 *Writings* 50 (1809) (First Inaugural Address). For John Calvin's views, see *Institutes of the Christian Religion,* 7th ed. (Philadelphia: Presbyterian Board of Christian Education, 1936), particularly Vol. 1, Book II, Ch. iii, pp. 317-319, and Ch. ii, p. 286. However, for a Calvinistic view more in tune with Madison's republicanism, see Calvin's views "On Civil Government" as developed in the last chapter of the *Institutes,* particularly the passage in Vol. 2, Book IV, Ch. xx, pp. 778-779, which begins: "The vice or imperfections of men therefore renders it safer and more tolerable for the government to be in the hands of the many. . . ."

22. *The Federalist,* Number 10, pp. 54, 55.

23. Ibid., p. 56.

24. Ibid.

25. Particularly 2 *Writings* 366-368 (1787) ("Vices . . ."); and *The Federalist,* Numbers 10 and 51.

26. 9 *Writings* 361 (1829) (Speech in the Virginia Constitutional Convention).

27. 5 *Writings* 28-29 (1787) (To Thomas Jefferson); and 9 *Writings* 526 (1833) (Memorandum on "Majority Governments"); *Debates,* pp. 168, 353-354; Madison's subsequent note on suffrage, pp. 619-623; 6 *Writings* 114-119 (1792) ("A Candid State of Parties," essay in *The National Gazette*).

28. All the "most enlightened and respectable citizens" would support a new, but just and stable, Constitution. *Debates,* p. 92. A right course, a right Constitution, would be approved by the "good sense" of the free, vigilant, manly, gallant citizens of America. *The Federalist,* Number 14, p. 84, Number 46, p. 311, Number 57, p. 373. And in the 1790s Madison emphasized the law-abiding character of the people (in connection with the Whiskey Rebellion), their "good sense and patriotism" in con-

nection with the scare created by the French Revolution, and their capability for rational self-government when enlightened, awakened, and united. 6 *Writings* 222-223 note (1794) (Speech in Congress); 6 *Writings* 118 and 120 (1792) (Essays in *The National Gazette*). Apropos the Hamiltonian-led Federalist party, Madison wrote to Jefferson that this party would not hesitate to use its power to establish in government a plutocratic stake-in-society theory, with "stockjobbers" becoming "the pretorian band of the Government, at once its tool and its tyrant; bribed by its largesse, and overawing it by clamours and combinations." 6 *Writings* 59 note (1791).

29. *The Federalist,* Number 55, p. 365.

30. 9 *Writings* 251 (1826) (To Henry Colman).

31. 5 *Writings* 223 (1788) (Speech in the Virginia Ratifying Convention).

32. *The Federalist,* Number 57, p. 373.

33. See *The Federalist,* Number 39, p. 343 and Number 63, pp. 409-410. For the abundant evidence to support the view of the more optimistic Madison, see *Debates,* p. 92; *The Federalist,* Number 46, p. 310, Number 55, pp. 362-363, Number 14, p. 84, Number 46, p. 311, Number 35, p. 373.

34. Thus Shays' insurgents were "malcontents" seeking "wicked measures." 2 *Writings* 354 (1787) (To Edmund Pendleton). Certain anti-Federalists were "ignorant and jealous men," "deluded opponents," and "designing leaders." 5 *Writings* 102 (1788) (To Thomas Jefferson) and 5 *Writings* 336 (1789) (To Thomas Jefferson). The Hamiltonians were anti-republicans. 5 *Writings* 120 and 116 (1792) (Essays in *The National Gazette*). For the stress on man's virtue, intelligence, and goodwill, see notes 28 and 36.

35. 6 *Writings* 85 (1792) ("Charters," essay in *The National Gazette*).

36. For Madison as a philosopher, compare the following: "In a Republic, light will prevail over darkness, truth over error: he had undoubted confidence in this principle"; 6 *Writings* 223 note (1794) (Speech in Congress); the "progress of light and freedom will not be halted"; 1 *Writings* 222 (1782) (To Edmund Randolph); nature will reassert its basic rights against tyranny and bigotry; 2 *Writings* 121 (1785) (To Marquis De Lafayette); the "rights of human nature" will be triumphant; 6 *Writings* 7 note (1790) (To Edmund Pendleton); the rule of "one paramount Empire of reason, benevolence, and brotherly affection" cannot long be held off; 6 *Writings* 69 (1791)

("Consolidation," essay in *The National Gazette*); "Knowledge will forever govern ignorance"; 9 *Writings* 103 (1822) (To W. T. Barry); "Despotism can only exist in darkness, and there are too many lights now in the political firmament, to permit it to reign anywhere, as it has hitherto, almost everywhere"; 9 *Writings* 35 (1820) (To Marquis De Lafayette).

Chapter 3

1. 2 *Writings* 361-369 (1787) ("Vices . . .").
2. See, for example, 1 *Writings* 58-59 (1780) (To James Madison, Sr.), 78 (1780) (To Joseph Jones), 93 (1780) (To Edmund Pendleton), 167-169 (1782) (To Edmund Pendleton), 382 note (1783) (Note to Speech in the Congress of the Confederation), 454-460 note (1783) ("Address to the States").
3. See 2 *Writings* 194-196 (1785) ("Notes for Speech in the Virginia House of Delegates"), 156-158 (1785) (To James Monroe), 162 (1785) (To Thomas Jefferson); and 1 *Writings* 465-467 note (1783) (To Edmund Randolph).
4. See 2 *Writings* 394-395, which contains Madison's 1835 sketch of the origin of the Constitutional Convention. For Madison's concern for the western frontier see, for example, 2 *Writings* 296-297 (1786) (To George Washington), 329-331 (1787) (To Thomas Jefferson); *Debates,* pp. 237 and 487; 5 *Writings* 179-184 (1788) (Speech in Virginia Ratifying Convention).
5. 2 *Writings* 394 (1835 constitutional sketch).
6. 2 *Writings* 396, and also 407-408.
7. See 2 *Writings* 313-316, 324-328, 336-340 (1787).
8. *Debates,* pp. 266, 371, 454; and 5 *Writings* 23 (1787) (To Thomas Jefferson).
9. *The Federalist,* Number 20, pp. 122-123; and Number 18, p. 112.
10. 2 *Writings* 326 (1787).
11. 5 *Writings* 19, 23, 27-28 (1787) (To Thomas Jefferson).
12. 5 *Writings* 126, 129, 138, 139, 145, 175 (1788) (Speech in Virginia Ratifying Convention).
13. 4 *Works* 273 (1833) (To Andrew Stevenson).
14. 9 *Writings* 357 note (1830) (To N. P. Trist). Vol. 9 of *Writings* and Vol. 4 of *Works* are abundantly full of this argument. Among the more important documents which make this point are Madison's comparable letters to Edward Everett, 9 *Writings* 383-403 (1830), and to Robert Y. Hayne, 383 note to 394 note (1830), and his lengthy "Notes on Nullification," 9 *Writings*

573-607 (1835). Madison's condemnation of nullification and secession runs throughout his correspondence after 1828.

15. 9 *Writings* 517 (1833) (To Henry Clay).
16. 9 *Writings* 577, 578 (1835) ("Notes on Nullification").
17. 9 *Writings* 525, 526, 528, 530 (1833) (Memorandum on "Majority Governments"). On the question of anarchy see also 9 *Writings* 575 (1833) ("Notes on Nullification").
18. 9 *Writings* 21-22 (1820).
19. 9 *Writings* 12 (1819) (To Robert Walsh).
20. 2 *Writings* 313-316, 324-328, 336-340 (1787).
21. 1 *Writings* 130 (1781) (To Thomas Jefferson); 2 *Writings* 180 (1785) (To Thomas Jefferson), 348 (1787) (To George Washington); and Madison's 1835 "Sketch," 2 *Writings* 408-409.
22. See, for example, 2 *Writings* 337-338 (1787) (To Edmund Randolph), 345 (1787) (To George Washington) where the idea of direct operation is still not explicit; *Debates,* pp. 256-257; and 5 *Writings* 19 (1787) (To Thomas Jefferson).
23. See Resolution 6 of the Virginia Plan, *Debates,* p. 24; 2 *Writings* 348 (1787) (To George Washington); and 5 *Writings* 19 (1787) (To Thomas Jefferson).
24. 2 *Writings* 346 (1787) (To George Washington); *Debates,* p. 24; and 2 *Writings* 346 (1787).
25. *Debates,* pp. 75-76, 266.
26. 5 *Writings* 19, 22-23, 26-27 (1787) (To Thomas Jefferson) and also Madison's 1835 "Sketch," 2 *Writings* 409.
27. 2 *Writings* 345-346; *Debates,* pp. 24, 570, 564.
28. *Debates,* pp. 479; 410-411, 557; 478.
29. See 2 *Writings* 347, 348-349 (1787) (To George Washington).
30. *Debates,* pp. 30, 73, 177, 193, 198, 256, 172, 401, 281, 95.
31. *Debates,* pp. 147, 487.
32. *Debates,* p. 301.
33. *Debates,* pp. 30-31, 70-71, 120-127, 177-180, 193-195, 198, 256-257.
34. 4 *Works* 357 (1834) (To Edward Coles).
35. Quoted in Irving Brant, *James Madison: Commander in Chief, 1812-1836* (Indianapolis: Bobbs-Merrill, 1961), p. 491.
36. 9 *Writings* 525 (1833) (Memorandum on "Majority Governments") and 9 *Writings* 575 (1833) ("Notes on Nullification").
37. See 9 *Writings* 432-433 (1831), 481-482 (1832), 520-528 (1833), 610 (1836); 4 *Works* 567-568 (1833), and 298 (1833).
38. For the speech in question see *Debates,* pp. 141-142. For the challenge to Madison later in life and his rebuttal, see 4 *Works*

209-210 (1831) (To N. P. Trist) and 280-289 (1835) (To John Tyler, but apparently unsent).
39. *The Federalist,* Number 45, p. 299; Number 46, p. 306.
40. *Debates,* p. 36.
41. See, for example, the second conclusion of *The Federalist,* Number 37, p. 232.
42. The charge was made by Senator John Tyler of Virginia. See 9 *Writings* 502-514 (1833) (Unsent letter to John Tyler).

Chapter 4

1. *The Federalist,* Number 39, p. 245.
2. Ibid., p. 250.
3. See K. C. Wheare, *Federal Government* (London: Oxford University Press, 1946).
4. *The Federalist,* Number 39, pp. 246-250.
5. *The Federalist,* Number 14, pp. 82-83. See also Number 39, pp. 248-249, and Number 45, p. 303.
6. *The Federalist,* Number 37, pp. 228-232.
7. *The Federalist,* Number 45, pp. 298-299.
8. *The Federalist,* Number 44, pp. 292-294.
9. Ibid., p. 295. See also Number 46, pp. 308-311, for more light on the "means of opposition" that might be employed to oppose "an unwarrantable measure of the federal government."
10. *The Federalist,* Number 46, p. 306.
11. 9 *Writings* 36 (1820); 3 *Works* 486 (1825) (To George Ticknor); 9 *Writings* 100 (1822) (To Edward Livingston); and *The Federalist,* Number 43, p. 285.
12. *The Federalist,* Number 39, p. 249; and 9 *Writings* 385-386 note (1830) (To Robert Y. Hayne). For Madison's claim that his position on the Court later in life was based in large part on what he had said in Number 39, see 9 *Writings* 397, 389-393 (1830) (To Edward Everett). Later in his life, Madison had reservations about the Supreme Court; yet on the essential point of the Court as an arbiter of the federal system—serving as a necessary if less effective device than a "federal negative" to avoid disunion—he held to the argument of Number 39 *Federalist.* See also his correspondence with Spencer Roane, 9 *Writings* 55-63, 65-68 (1821); and 9 *Writings* 606-607 (1835) ("Notes on Nullification").
13. *The Federalist,* Number 14, p. 84; Number 43, p. 288.
14. This point of view runs throughout W. W. Crosskey, *Politics and the Constitution,* 2 vols. (Chicago: University of Chicago

Press, 1953). For a sample of Crosskey's view of Madison's early high nationalism, see I, 187, 191-192, 221-223 (commerce power), 406 (general welfare and common defense), 197 (President's removal power), 664-665 (positive and complete authority in all cases requiring uniformity), 682 (power by implication), 688-690 (Tenth Amendment); II, 985 (Supremacy Clause). For a sample of Crosskey's charges of Madison's "apostasy" on the question of national power, the difference between Madison's public and private views, devious ways, dishonesty, inconsistency, trickery, bluffing, see I, 404-405, 401, 406, 410-411, 197, 369-370, 509, 644-645, 690.

For a brief critique of Crosskey, in defense of Madison, see Stuart Gerry Brown, *The First Republicans: Political Philosophy and Public Policy in the Party of Jefferson and Madison* (Syracuse: Syracuse University Press, 1954), Appendix, pp. 176-186. I am in general agreement with Brown's "Observations on Crosskey's Politics and the Constitution." It is perhaps unnecessary to point out that Irving Brant's biography does not support Crosskey's charges. For Brant's critique of Crosskey, see "Mr. Crosskey and Mr. Madison," *Columbia Law Review,* 54, No. 3 (March, 1954), 443-450. In this same issue Julius Gobel, Jr., Professor of Legal History at Columbia Law School, also criticizes Crosskey; while Malcolm Sharp of the Chicago Law School takes a more favorable view of Crosskey's book. With Brant, I regret that the sound work in Crosskey's book may be marred by his attempt to twist the facts with regard to Madison.

15. A Southern interpretation of interposition is Committee for Courts of Justice, Senate of Virginia, *The Doctrine of Interposition: Its History and Application* (Richmond: Division of Purchase and Printing, 1957). The Virginia Resolution on Interposition, adopted February 1, 1956, may be found in *Race Relations Law Reporter,* 1, No. 2 (April, 1956), 445-447.

16. *The Federalist,* Number 39, p. 250.

17. See particularly Madison's speech against the bank bill, 6 *Writings* 29-34 (1791) and the report on the Virginia Resolutions, 6 *Writings* 383-385 (1799-1800).

18. 6 *Writings* 28 (1791) (Speech in First Congress); 6 *Writings* 354-357 (1799-1800) (Report on the Virginia Resolutions).

19. For the text of this speech—magnificent in its splendid isolation—see *Debates,* pp. 111-120. Hamilton was "unfriendly" to both the Virginia and New Jersey plans. Presumably, Hamilton favored a unitary government (what he called a "general gov-

ernment"); but although he recognized that great economy might be achieved by extinguishing state governments, he "did not mean however to shock the public opinion by proposing such a measure." State governments were "not necessary for any of the great purposes of commerce, revenue, or agriculture," although "Subordinate authorities" were necessary for "local purposes." He candidly admitted that "the British Government was the best in the world" and "doubted much whether anything short of it would do in America." His Senate would consist of men elected to serve during good behavior. His Chief Executive would similarly serve during good behavior. And better to ensure that all laws of the particular states contrary to the Constitution or laws of the United States be utterly void, he suggested the Governor of each state be appointed by the "General Government" and have a "negative upon the laws to be passed in the State." He despaired of the possibility of establishing republican government over such a large country.

20. See, for example, 9 *Writings* 574, 575, 606-607, 586, 583, 578 ("Notes on Nullification"); and 9 *Writings* 395-398, 388-389, 389-394 (To Edward Everett).
21. 4 *Works* 357 (1834) (To Edward Coles).
22. 9 *Writings* 577-578, 581, 597, 589 (1835) "Notes on Nullification").
23. 9 *Writings* 431-433 (1831) (To Reynolds Chapman), 4 *Works* 196 (1831) (To Joseph C. Cabell), 261, 264 (1832) (Unsent letter to Professor John A. G. Davis), 568 (1833) (To Henry Clay), 357-358 (1834) (To Edward Coles), 9 *Writings* 357 note (1830) (To N. P. Trist); 9 *Writings* 481-482 (1832) (Paper enclosed in letter to N. P. Trist), and 4 *Works* 567-568 (1833) (To Henry Clay); 9 *Writings* 525-527 (1833) (Memorandum on "Majority Governments"); 9 *Writings* 610 (1836) (Probably unsent letter; not addressed), and 4 *Works* 298 (1833) (To Benjamin F. Papoon).
24. *The Federalist,* Number 14, p. 85.

Chapter 5

1. 2 *Writings* 164 (1787).
2. 5 *Writings* 176 (1788).
3. 5 *Writings* 31 (1787); and 2 *Writings* 123 (1785) (To Marquis De Lafayette).
4. *The Federalist,* Number 10, pp. 53-54.

5. Ibid., pp. 55-56; and 5 *Writings* 28-29 (1787) (To Thomas Jefferson).

6. 2 *Writings* 366 (1787) ("Vices. . ."); and *The Federalist,* Number 10, pp. 54, 56-57.

7. *The Federalist,* Number 10, pp. 57-58.

8. 5 *Writings* 31 (1787) (To Thomas Jefferson); *The Federalist,* Number 10, pp. 54-55, 57, 58.

9. See, for example, 2 *Writings* 366-367 (1787) ("Vices. . ."), *Debates,* pp. 64-65, *The Federalist,* Number 51, 5 *Writings* 27-32 (1787) (To Thomas Jefferson); and *The Federalist,* Number 10, pp. 58, 59.

10. *The Federalist,* Number 10, p. 53.

11. Ibid., p. 54.

12. Ibid., p. 62.

13. Charles Beard, *An Economic Interpretation of the Constitution* (1913; New York: Macmillan, 1935), p. 324. For Beard's appraisal of Madison on this point, see Beard's comment on p. 125. Madison's own ethical rule can be found in Douglass Adair, ed., "James Madison's Autobiography," *William and Mary Quarterly,* Third Series, II (April, 1945), 203-204.

14. See, for example, 2 *Writings* 368 (1787) ("Vices. . ."), *Debates,* p. 65, *The Federalist,* Number 10, pp. 61-62, 5 *Writings* 27-32 (1787) (To Thomas Jefferson); and 6 *Writings* 70 (1792) ("Public Opinion," essay in *The National Gazette*).

15. David Truman, *The Governmental Process* (New York: Alfred A. Knopf, 1951), pp. 37, 55, has noted that the revolution in communication and travel has "rendered largely obsolete" "Madison's confidence in the dispersion of the population as an obstacle to the formulation of interest groups."

16. In 1787 party and faction are hardly distinguishable in Madison's writings. By 1792 in his essay on "Parties" in *The National Gazette,* a slight distinction is made between party and interest, although parties are still held to be evil, if—like interests—unavoidable. 6 *Writings* 86 (1792). By the end of 1792 in an essay, "A Candid State of Parties," Madison's reflection on the history and state of the parties in America had led him to conclude that there is a distinction between good and bad parties, republican and anti-republican parties. 6 *Writings* 106-119 (1792). Apparently, Madison had been forced to defend the Republican party against the charge that it constituted a faction. The actuality and success of the Republican party convinced him of the value of the right kind of party, although he still harbored deep suspicion of the wrong kind of party. See 9

Writings 190 (1824) (To Henry Lee), where Madison also states that parties "seem to have a permanent foundation in the variance of political opinions in free states, and of occupations and interests in all civilized States."

17. *The Federalist,* Number 10, pp. 59-60; 2 *Writings* 369 (1787) ("Vices. . ."). Madison's views on the role of the representative are implicit in *The Federalist.* They are stated more explicitly in 3 *Works* 478-479 (1824) (To Henry Lee) and in 4 *Works* 428-429 (1836) (To _____ _____). See also "Madison's 'Detached Memoranda,' " *William and Mary Quarterly,* Third Series, III (October, 1946), 562-564, *Debates,* p. 92, and 1 *Writings* 340 (1783) (Speech in the Congress of the Confederation).

18. *The Federalist,* Number 10, p. 363, Numbers 14 and 51, and 9 *Writings* 521 (1833) (Memorandum on "Majority Governments").

19. *The Federalist,* Number 51, pp. 340-341: "In the extended republic of the United States, and among the great variety of interests, parties, and sects which it embraces, a coalition of a majority of the whole society could seldom take place on any other principles than those of justice and the general good. . . ."

20. *The Federalist,* Number 10, p. 60.

21. *The Federalist,* Number 44, pp. 289-291.

22. Ibid., p. 291; and 6 *Writings* 101-103 (1792) ("Property," essay in *The National Gazette*), 5 *Writings* 437-441 note (1790) (To Thomas Jefferson).

23. *The Federalist,* Number 51, p. 337; and also Number 57, pp. 373-374.

24. The quoted material may be found in *The Federalist,* Number 10, p. 56, 2 *Writings* 368 (1787) ("Vices. . ."), and *The Federalist,* Number 48, p. 321.

25. For Madison's views in the Convention, see *Debates,* pp. 167-168, 556.

26. The Senate was "to protect the people against their rulers" and "to protect the people against the transient impressions into which they themselves might be led." A knowledgeable, enlightened, calm Senate would protect the integrity of republican government, particularly against the "leveling spirit" and the "true danger" of the "agrarian attempts" produced by economic class struggle. A wise, virtuous Senate could aid in such future emergencies by throwing its weight into the scale on the side of justice. Such a Senate would provide a safeguard against the defects of republican government. *Debates,* pp. 167-168.

Madison's objective thus was the protection of republican government which could be threatened by both the rich and the poor when either deviated from the principles of justice. For Madison's understanding of property, see his essay on "Property," in 6 *Writings* 101-103 (1792), and on "Monopolies, Perpetuities, Corporations, Ecclesiastical Endowments," *William and Mary Quarterly,* Third Series, III (October, 1946), 551-562. On the double-edged sword of oppression, see Madison's speeches on suffrage where this point emerges most clearly.

27. *Debates,* pp. 111-120; and 2 *Writings* 346-347 (1787) (To George Washington), 368 (1787) ("Vices. . ."). For Madison's speech on the removal power of the President, see 5 *Writings* 361-365 (1789). However, for a narrower view of Presidential power, particularly in foreign affairs, see "Letters of Helvidius," in 6 *Writings.*

28. See, for example, 9 *Writings* 520-528 (1833) (Memorandum on "Majority Governments").

29. See, for example, *Debates,* pp. 353-354 (where Madison's conflicting sentiments on suffrage are reflected), *Debates,* pp. 619-623 (for his subsequent views), 5 *Writings* 286-287 (1788) ("Observations on the 'Draught of a Constitution for Virginia' "), and 9 *Writings* 358-364 (1829) (Speech in the Virginia Constitutional Convention).

30. *Debates,* pp. 353-354, 619-623, particularly p. 623.

Chapter 6

1. See, for example, 1 *Writings* 93 (1780) (To Edmund Pendleton); 2 *Writings* 319 (1787) (To Edmund Pendleton), 326 (1787) (To Thomas Jefferson), 340 (1787) (To Edmund Randolph); *Debates,* pp. 95-96; 5 *Writings* 197 (1788) (Speech in the Virginia Ratifying Convention).

2. *Debates,* pp. 95-96.

3. 5 *Writings* 398-402 (? 1835) ("Sketch" of the Origin of the Constitutional Convention).

4. 1 *Works* 339 (1787).

5. *The Federalist,* Number 40, p. 259.

6. *The Federalist,* Number 40, pp. 257-258; and Number 43, p. 287.

7. 2 *Writings* 183-191 (1785) ("Memorial and Remonstrance Against Religious Assessments"); and 2 *Writings* 216 (1786).

8. 2 *Writings* 185-186 (1785) ("Memorial and Remonstrance Against Religious Assessments").

9. *The Federalist,* Number 51, p. 337; and Number 57, p. 370.

10. See, for example, Madison's speeches in the Virginia Ratifying Convention, 5 *Writings* 123-234 (1788), particularly pp. 132, 176, 228-234; 5 *Writings* 271-275 (1788) (To Thomas Jefferson), 319-321 note (1789) (To George Eye), 370-389 (1789) (Speech in Congress on Amendments to the Constitution).

11. 5 *Writings* 370-389 (1789) (Speech in Congress on Amendments to the Constitution).

12. 6 *Writings* 113-116 (1792) ("A Candid State of Parties," essay in *The National Gazette*); and 6 *Writings* 120 and 122 (1792) ("Who Are the Best Keepers of the People's Liberties?"—essay in *The National Gazette*).

13. The exact quote is in 6 *Writings* 327 (1798) (Virginia Resolutions of 1798).

14. 6 *Writings* 328-329 (1798) (Virginia Resolutions of 1798).

15. See 6 *Writings* 108-119 (1792) for the substance of Madison's conversation with President Washington, as it relates to Madison's suspicions of the Federalist party. On the Whiskey Rebellion and Madison's criticism of Washington, see 6 *Writings* 220-224 (1794) (To James Monroe). On the French Revolution, Genêt, and partisan politics, see 6 *Writings* 188-190 (1793) (To Archibald Stuart), and 190-195 (1793) (To Thomas Jefferson).

16. 9 *Writings* 520, 526 (1833) (Memorandum on "Majority Governments").

17. See, for example, Madison's essays on "Public Opinion," "Who Are the Best Keepers of the People's Liberties?" in 6 *Writings* 70, 120-123 (1792); 6 *Writings* 328-329 (1798) (Virginia Resolutions of 1798), 393-398 (1799-1800) (Report on the Virginia Resolutions); 9 *Writings* 231-232 (1825) (To Thomas Ritchie); 6 *Writings* 83-85 (1792) ("Charter," essay in *The National Gazette*); 9 *Writings* 101 (1822) (To Edward Livingston); 6 *Writings* 87 (1792) ("British Government," essay in *The National Gazette*).

18. 6 *Writings* 179 note (1793) (To Thomas Jefferson).

19. 6 *Writings* 70 (1792) ("Public Opinion," essay in *The National Gazette*).

20. 6 *Writings* 86 (1792) ("British Government," essay in *The National Gazette*). See also 3 *Works* 142 (1819) (To Richard Bland Lee): "Political parties intermingled throughout the community unite as well as divide every section of it."

21. See Madison's Virginia Resolutions of 1798, 6 *Writings* 326-331 (1798); his "Address of the General Assembly to the People of the Commonwealth of Virginia," 6 *Writings* 332-340 (1799);

and his lengthy report on the Virginia Resolutions, 6 *Writings* 341-406 (1799-1800).

22. Constitutional argument, of course, was the technique Madison had employed against the first bank bill. This now orthodox technique, he felt, should always be used in the first instance to oppose and defeat anti-republican measures. See 9 *Writings* 597 (1835) ("Notes on Nullification"), where Madison proposed to rely initially upon "the checks provided among the constituted authorities"—that is, the legislators in House and Senate, the President, the courts.

23. 6 *Writings* 331, 326, 321 (1798) (Virginia Resolutions of 1798), 401-403 (1799-1800) (Report on the Virginia Resolutions); 9 *Writings* 402, 403 (1830) (To Edward Everett).

24. See 9 *Writings* 574, 582, including note 1, 594-597, including note 1 on p. 594 (1835) ("Notes on Nullification").

25. 9 *Writings* 575, 583, 592, 597-599, 606-607 (1835) ("Notes on Nullification").

26. Ibid., 576, 579, 580.

27. Ibid., 573-574, 575, 588-591, 604.

28. Ibid., 597.

29. Quite obviously, Madison in 1835 was trying to put the Virginia Resolutions in the best possible light. Although I believe that his argument on behalf of ultraconstitutional interposition is ambiguous in several important respects, and that he was clearly taking a stronger line against alleged states' rights in 1835 than in 1798 and 1799, I am convinced that his central argument—that South Carolina's doctrine of nullification cannot be fathered on the Virginia Resolutions—is correct.

30. 9 *Writings* 231-232 (1825) (To Thomas Ritchie). See also 9 *Writings* 287 (1827) (To Joseph C. Cabell), 327 note (1828) (To Joseph C. Cabell); and 4 *Works* 72-73 (1830) (To Edward Everett). Madison also stressed the distinction between "the case of a law *confessedly* unconstitutional, and a case turning on a *doubt* and a *divided opinion* as to the meaning of the Constitution. . . ."

31. See, for example, 9 *Writings* 316-340 (1828) (To Joseph C. Cabell) for Madison's views on the constitutionality of the tariff; and also Madison's unsent letter to Professor John A. G. Davis in 4 *Works* 232-266 (1832), which expressed more fully and systematically the position he took on the tariff elsewhere. On what was required to heal the sectional breach, see 9 *Writings* 432-433 (1831) (To Reynolds Chapman), 481-482 (1832) (paper enclosed in letter to N. P. Trist), 520-528 (Memo-

randum on "Majority Governments"), 610 (1836) (To _____
_____); 4 *Works* 567-568 (1833) (To Henry Clay), 298
(1833) (To Benjamin F. Papoon).
32. 6 *Writings* 85 (1792) ("Charters," essay in *The National Gazette*).

Chapter 7

1. See Neal Riemer, *The Revival of Democratic Theory* (New
York: Appleton-Century-Crofts, 1962), and *The Future of the
Democratic Revolution: Toward a More Prophetic Politics*
(New York: Praeger, 1984). For my attempt to place Madison
in the larger context of American political theory in its forma-
tive period, see *The Democratic Experiment* (Princeton: Van
Nostrand, 1967).

Bibliographical Essay

Those who want to pursue Madison's political theory in the context of his rich life and times may wisely begin with Irving Brant's splendid, sympathetic but critical six-volume biography, which, more than any other work, has restored Madison to a preeminent place in American history. See *James Madison: The Virginia Revolutionist, 1751-1780* (1941); *James Madison: The Nationalist, 1780-1787* (1948); *James Madison: Father of the Constitution, 1787-1800* (1950); *James Madison: Secretary of State, 1800-1809* (1953); *James Madison: The President, 1809-1812* (1956); and *James Madison: Commander in Chief, 1812-1836* (1961) (Indianapolis: Bobbs-Merrill). For Brant's one-volume biography of Madison, see *The Fourth President: A Life of James Madison* (Indianapolis: Bobbs-Merrill, 1970). See also Brant, *James Madison and American Nationalism* (Princeton: Van Nostrand, 1968). Two additional articles by Brant may also serve to correct the distortions of such earlier historians as Henry Adams and such modern critics as W. W. Crosskey. See "James Madison and His Times," *American Historical Review,* LVII, No. 4 (July, 1952), 853-870, and "Mr. Crosskey and Mr. Madison," *Columbia Law Review,* 54 (March, 1954), 443-450.

For additional, up-to-date, one-volume biographies, see Ralph Ketcham, *James Madison: A Biography* (New York: Macmillan, 1970); Harold S. Schultz, *James Madison* (New York: Twayne, 1971); Robert A. Rutland, *James Madison and the Search for Nationhood* (Washington, D.C.: Library of Congress, 1981). See also Merrill D. Peterson, ed., *James Madison: A Biography in His Own Words* (New York: Newsweek/Harper & Row, 1974), which is based on William T. Hutchinson et al., eds., *The Papers of James Madison* (see p.

192 for fuller data on this series).

The brilliant historical detective work of Douglass Adair has greatly helped to illuminate Madison's intellectual antecedents, his relation to Jeffersonian Democracy, the authorship of *The Federalist,* and other matters relevant to Madison's political theory. See "The Intellectual Origins of Jeffersonian Democracy" (unpublished Ph.D. thesis, Yale University, 1943); "That Politics May Be Reduced to a Science: David Hume, James Madison, and the Tenth Federalist," *The Huntington Library Quarterly,* XX, No. 4 (August, 1957), 343-360; "The Authorship of the Disputed Federalist Papers," *William and Mary Quarterly,* Third Series, I (April and July, 1944), 97-122, 235-264; and "The Tenth Federalist Revisited," *William and Mary Quarterly,* Third Series, VIII (January, 1951), 48-61. Adair's important essays may also be found in *Fame and the Founding Fathers* (New York: Norton, 1974).

On other intellectual antecedents and the climate of opinion influencing Madison and his generation, see the revealing work of Caroline Robbins, *The Eighteenth-Century Commonwealthman: Studies in the Transmission, Development, and Circumstances of English Liberal Thought from the Restoration of Charles II until the War with the Thirteen Colonies* (Cambridge, Mass.: Harvard University Press, 1959), and of H. Trevor Colbourne, *The Lamp of Experience: Whig History and the Intellectual Origins of the American Revolution* (Chapel Hill: University of North Carolina Press, 1965). See also J. G. A. Pocock, *The Machiavellian Moment: Florentine Political Thought and Atlantic Republican Tradition* (Princeton: Princeton University Press, 1975), and his *Virtue, Commerce, and History: Essays on Political Thought and History, Chiefly in the Eighteenth Century* (New York: Cambridge University Press, 1985). Most helpful, too, are the bibliographical essays by Robert E. Shalhope, "Toward a Republican Synthesis: The Emergence of Republicanism in American Historiography," *William and Mary Quarterly,* Third Series, XXIX (January, 1972), 49-80, and "Republicanism and Early American Historiography," *William and Mary Quarterly,* Third Series, XXXIX (April, 1982), 334-356.

Two studies brilliantly illuminating the thought of the revolutionary and constitutional generations are Bernard Bailyn, *Ideological Origins of the American Revolution* (Cambridge, Mass.: Harvard University Press, 1967), and Gordon Wood, *The Creation of the American Republic* (Chapel Hill: University of North Carolina Press, 1969). Robert R. Palmer, *The Age of the Democratic Revolution: A Political History of Europe and America, 1760-1800,* 2 vols. (Princeton: Princeton University Press, 1959, 1964) helps one to see Madison's accomplishment in a larger comparative perspective. Clinton Rossiter, *The Seedtime of the Republic: The Origin of the American Tradition of Political Liberty* (New York: Harcourt Brace, 1953) splendidly brings the early republican ferment to life.

The writings of Adrienne Koch have also helped us to understand better Madison's political philosophy as it agreed with and differed from that of his friend Jefferson and his fellow philosopher-statesmen of the republic, Alexander Hamilton and John Adams. See, particularly, her *Jefferson and Madison: The Great Collaboration* (New York: Alfred A. Knopf, 1950); *Madison's "Advice To My Country"* (Princeton: Princeton University Press, 1966); *Powers, Morals and the Founding Fathers* (Ithaca, N.Y.: Great Seal Books, Cornell University Press, 1961); and "James Madison and the Empire of Liberty," *The Review of Politics,* XIV (January, 1954), 37-66.

An earlier book-length study of Madison's political thought is Edward McNall Burns, *James Madison: Philosopher of the Constitution* (New Brunswick, N.J.: Rutgers University Press, 1938). This work helpfully analyzes Madison's ideas on a number of key subjects, but it was written before the research of Brant and Adair. Another excellent study that deals with Madison's political philosophy and that of his fellow Republicans is Stuart Gerry Brown, *The First Republicans: Political Philosophy and Public Policy in the Party of Jefferson and Madison* (Syracuse: Syracuse University Press, 1954). A fresh study, full of insights, is Gary Wills, *Explaining America: The Federalist* (Garden City, N.Y.: Doubleday, 1981). This book is, however, limited to *The Federalist* and does not explore Madison's thought in the

1790s or later. Wills' study is one in his brilliant, and much needed, series on "The American Enlightenment." Wills follows Adair's lead in attributing great influence on *The Federalist* to David Hume. A source-book and commentary on Madison is Marvin Meyers, ed., *The Mind of the Founder: Sources of the Political Thought of James Madison,* rev. ed. (Hanover, N.H.: University Press of New England, 1981). See also the work of Martin Diamond on *The Federalist,* especially *The Founding of the Democratic Republic* (Itasca, Ill.: Peacock, 1981). The thoughtful study by David F. Epstein, *The Political Theory of "The Federalist"* (Chicago: University of Chicago Press, 1984) considers "both why and how *The Federalist* proposes to combine liberalism with a 'strictly republican' form of government" (p. 7). Vincent Ostrom, *The Political Theory of a Compound Republic: A Reconstruction of the Logical Foundations of American Democracy in "The Federalist"* (Blacksburg: Virginia Polytechnic Institute, 1971), argues that the political theory of a compound republic "implies ... a theory of concurrent regimes, which ... represents the most important innovation in political theory since the rise of the nation-state ..." (p. 2). For a series of illuminating essays attempting "to clarify the elements involved in that important part of constitutional interpretation which is based upon different conceptions of democracy" (p. 1), see Martin Edelman, ed., *Democratic Theories and the Constitution* (Albany: State University of New York Press, 1984).

My own Madisonian research and criticism, most of it predating the first edition of this book in 1968, may be found in the following articles: "The Republicanism of James Madison," *Political Science Quarterly,* LXIX (March, 1954), 45-64; "James Madison's Theory of the Self-Destructive Features of Republican Government," *Ethics,* LXV (October, 1954), 34-43; "James Madison and the Current Conservative Vogue," *The Antioch Review,* XIV (Winter, 1954-55), 458-470; "Two Conceptions of the Genius of American Politics," *Journal of Politics,* 20 (November, 1958), 695-717; "Political Theory as a Guide to Action: Madison and the Prudential Component in Politics," *Social Science,* 35 (January, 1960), 17-25; and "Creative Breakthroughs in Politics," *The Journal of Political Inquiry,* II (No. 1, 1974), 1-22. My own effort to place Madison in the American democratic tradition—and to relate him to major men and movements in his lifetime—will be found in my book *The Democratic Experiment* (Princeton: Van Nostrand, 1967). For my argument, using Madison (and Jefferson) to illustrate the prophetic tradition in American politics, see *The Future of the Democratic Revolution: Toward a More Prophetic Politics* (New York: Praeger, 1984).

For the anti-Federalist response to Madison's republican dilemma—that of attempting to reconcile republican liberty and authority to govern in a country of large size—see the important article by Cecelia M. Kenyon, "Men of Little Faith: The Anti-Federalists on the Nature of Representative Government," *William and Mary Quarterly,* Third Series, XII (January, 1955), 3-43. Professor Kenyon elaborates on this theme in the Introduction of her edition of *The Anti-Federalists* (Indianapolis: Bobbs-Merrill, 1966). The anti-Federalist theory that emerges provides a striking contrast to Madison's own political theory. For another helpful understanding, see Robert A. Rutland, *The Ordeal of the Constitution: The Anti-Federalists and the Ratification Struggle of 1787-1788* (Norman: University of Oklahoma Press, 1966).

For the debate about Madison's strong nationalism in 1787—and his subsequent alleged heretical backsliding—see the very one-sided conspiracy theory in W. W. Crosskey, *Politics and the Constitution of the United States,* 2 vols. (Chicago: University of Chicago Press, 1953). In addition to Brant's critique of Crosskey mentioned near the beginning of this essay, one may find another pro-Madison critique in the Appendix of Stuart Gerry Brown, *The First Republicans: Political Philosophy and Public Policy in the Party of Jefferson and Madison* (Syracuse: Syracuse University Press, 1954). For a judicious appraisal of the United States under the Articles of Confederation, see Richard B. Morris, "The Confederation Period and the American Historian," *William and Mary Quarterly,* Third Series, XIII (April, 1956), 139-156. Merrill Jensen has done a great deal to revise the exaggerations of earlier writers about the "critical period" of American history—the period prior to the adoption of the Constitution—but he does not explicitly refute Madison's analysis of the vices that plagued the American system prior to 1787. See three of Jensen's books: *The Articles of Confederation: An Interpretation of the Social-Constitutional History of the American Revolution, 1774-1781* (Madison: University of Wisconsin Press, 1940); *The New Nation: A History of the United States During the Confederation, 1781-1789* (New York: Alfred A. Knopf, 1950); and *The Making of the American Constitution* (Princeton: Van Nostrand, 1964).

Modern writers aware of the problems facing the new nations of Asia and Africa tend to be more sympathetic to the nationalism of 1787. See Seymour Martin Lipset, *The First New Nation: The United States in Historical and Comparative Perspective* (New York: Basic Books, 1963). For the crucial period between Revolution and Constitution, see also Benjamin F. Wright's judicious appraisal: *Consensus and Continuity, 1776-1787* (Boston: Boston University Press, 1958).

If one assumes that political theory is a crass, or sophisticated, response to economic forces, one will be interested in the literature centering on an economic interpretation of the Constitution. To my knowledge few have indicted Madison personally for writing his private economic interests into his political theory. This, of course, is not to say that Madison's economic and social position did not influence his thinking; nor is it to say that Madison did not recognize the intimate connection between economics and politics. The forces shaping Madison's political theory were primarily political and moral—liberty, justice, union—and his theory was not designed to ensure the perpetual supremacy of his economic class. He was no Marx of the Master Class. For a sampling of the literature one may profitably start with Cecelia M. Kenyon, "An Economic Interpretation of the Constitution After Fifty Years," *The Centennial Review,* VII (Summer, 1963), 327-352. Then one can turn to the literature, pro and con: Charles A. Beard, *An Economic Interpretation of the Constitution* (New York: Macmillan, 1913); Robert E. Brown, *Charles Beard and the Constitution: A Critical Analysis of "An Economic Interpretation of the Constitution"* (Princeton: Princeton University Press, 1956); Forrest McDonald, *We The People: The Economic Origins of the Constitution*

(Chicago: University of Chicago Press, 1958); and Jackson Turner Main, "Charles Beard and the Constitution: A Critical Review of Forrest McDonald's *We the People,* with a Rebuttal by Forrest McDonald," *William and Mary Quarterly,* Third Series, XVII (January, 1960), 86-110.

For the literature on federalism, and Madison's contribution, see the following: Gottfried Dietze's comprehensive account in *The Federalist: A Classic on Federalism and Free Government* (Baltimore: Johns Hopkins Press, 1960); Alpheus T. Mason, "The Federalist—A Split Personality," *American Historical Review,* LVII (April, 1952), 625-643; Samuel Huntington, "The Founding Fathers and the Division of Powers," in Arthur Maass, ed., *Area and Power* (Glencoe, Ill.: Free Press, 1959); Charles H. McIlwain, "The Historical Background of Federal Government," in Roscoe Pound et al., *Federalism as a Democratic Process* (New Brunswick, N.J.: Rutgers University Press, 1942); K. C. Wheare, *Federal Government,* 5th ed. (Westport, Conn.: Greenwood Press, 1984); and Walter H. Bennett, *American Theories of Federalism* (University: University of Alabama Press, 1964). Dietze emphasizes that *The Federalist* advocated federalism as a means to achieve security in the world and peace among the states in the nation, and especially to advance individual freedom from governmental control. Wheare argues that federalism is a response to large size. See also Gary Wills, *Explaining America: The Federalist* (Garden City, N.Y.: Doubleday, 1981), and Martin Diamond, *The Founding of the Democratic Republic* (Itasca, Ill.: Peacock, 1981), both mentioned earlier.

For additional literature on what I have called Madison's theory of the extensive republic, see especially Vincent Ostrom, *The Political Theory of a Compound Republic: A Reconstruction of the Logical Foundations of American Democracy in "The Federalist"* (Blacksburg: Virginia Polytechnic Institute, 1971), and Gary Wills, *Explaining America: The Federalist,* particularly chapters 26-29. See also those writings in the pluralist tradition from Arthur F. Bentley, *The Process of Government* (1908; Cambridge, Mass.: Belknap Press of Harvard University Press, 1967) to David Truman, *The Governmental Process* (New York: Alfred A. Knopf, 1951) and Robert A. Dahl, *Pluralist Democracy in the*

United States: Conflict and Consent (Chicago: Rand McNally, 1967). In *A Preface to Democratic Theory* (Chicago: University of Chicago Press, 1956), Dahl contrasts a "Madisonian Model" of democracy (based primarily on the principle of separation of powers and checks and balances) to a populist model (majority rule) and to a pluralist model (Dahl's own empirical choice). Unhappily, Dahl's "Madisonian Model" is not based accurately on the full historical theory of James Madison. A comparable adverse criticism of Madison's theory—as much normative as empirical—is to be found in James MacGregor Burns, *The Deadlock of Democracy: Four-Party Politics in America* (Englewood Cliffs, N.J.: Prentice-Hall, 1963). A more sympathetic and balanced account of Madison is to be found in Burns' highly readable *The Vineyard of Liberty* (New York: Random House, 1982). The negativism often traced to Madison's belief in separation of powers and checks and balances is really attributable more to his pluralistic premise: it will be difficult for the many interests in a large federal country to unite and carry out their plans. Dahl does not appreciate that Madison's historical theory rested primarily upon the reality of a large country, multiple and diverse interests, and representation, and not upon such formal constitutional devices as separation of powers and checks and balances. A more balanced understanding of Madison's theory, contribution, and relevance is to be found in Arthur H. Holcombe, *Our More Perfect Union: From Eighteenth Century Principles to Twentieth Century Practice* (Cambridge, Mass.: Harvard University Press, 1950).

For a few additional books on federalism, see Carl J. Friedrich, *Trends of Federalism in Theory and Practice* (New York: Praeger, 1968); George Benson, *Essays in Federalism* (Claremont, Calif.: Claremont Men's College, 1966); Robert A. Goldwin, ed., *A Nation of States* (Chicago: Rand McNally, 1963); Daniel J. Elazar, *American Federalism: A View from the States,* 3rd ed. (New York: Harper & Row, 1984); and William Riker, *Federalism: Origin, Operation, Significance* (Boston: Little, Brown, 1964). See also the many excellent articles in *Publius: The Journal of Federalism.*

For additional literature relevant to what I have called Madison's theory of democratic politics, one may profitably consult James Morton Smith's scholarly and exciting *Freedom's Fetters: The Alien and Sedition Laws and American Civil Liberties* (Ithaca, N.Y.: Cornell University Press, 1958); David Spitz' carefully reasoned *Democracy and the Challenge of Power* (New York: Columbia University Press, 1958); Arthur E. Sutherland, *Constitutionalism in America: Origin and Evolution of Its Fundamental Ideas* (Waltham, Mass.: Blaisdell, 1966); Bernard Schwartz, *The Great Rights of Mankind* (New York: Oxford University Press, 1977); Joyce Appleby, *Capitalism and a New Social Order: The Republican Vision of the 1790s* (New York: New York University Press, 1984); Noble E. Cunningham, Jr., *The Jeffersonian Republicans in Power: The Formation of Party Organization, 1789-1801* (Chapel Hill: University of North Carolina Press, 1957); Richard Hofstader, *The Idea of a Party System, 1780-1840* (Berkeley: University of California Press, 1969); John Zvesper, *Political Philosophy and Rhetoric: A Study of the Origins of American Party Politics* (London: Cambridge University Press, 1977); Joseph Charles, *The Origins of the American Party System* (Williamsburg, Va.: Institute of Early American History and Culture, 1956); William Nesbit Chambers, *Political Parties in a New Nation: The American Experience, 1776-1809* (New York: Oxford University Press, 1963); Harry Ammon, "The Republican Party in Virginia: 1789-1824" (unpublished Ph.D. thesis, University of Virginia, 1948); and Frank J. Sorauf, *Party Politics in America,* 5th ed. (Boston: Little, Brown, 1984). A study focusing on Madison's evolving political theory, and democratic politics, remains to be written.

For literature on the War of 1812, see especially Robert A. Rutland, *Madison's Alternatives: The Jeffersonian Republicans and the Coming of War, 1805-1812* (Philadelphia: Lippincott, 1975), and J. C. A. Stagg, *Mr. Madison's War: Politics, Diplomacy, and Warfare in the Early American Republic, 1783-1830* (Princeton: Princeton University Press, 1983). Stagg sees the War of 1812 as a "demanding trial of all the issues and assumptions that were at the heart of post-independence American politics" (p. xi). A study remains to be written of Madison's political theory and the War of 1812.

Those who want to sample primary Madisonian sources may turn to the splendid volumes in the ongoing project *The Papers of James Madison,* originally edited by William T. Hutchinson and William M. E. Rachal, and now edited by Robert A. Rutland and Charles F. Hobson. As of 1986, fifteen volumes have been published by the University of Chicago Press and the University of Virginia Press. Volume 15 extends through April 20, 1795. In my own research, which predated this edition, I relied upon Gaillard Hunt's edition of *The Writings of James Madison,* 9 vols. (New York: G. P. Putnam's Sons, 1900-1910); *Madison's Works: Letters and Other Writings of James Madison,* 4 vols. (New York: R. Worthington, 1884); and the one-volume Gaillard Hunt-J. B. Scott edition of Madison's notes, *The Debates in the Federal Convention of 1787* (New York: Oxford University Press, 1920). Madison's account of the debates has recently been republished with an Introduction by Adrienne Koch: *Notes of Debates in the Federal Convention of 1787 Reported by James Madison* (Athens: Ohio University Press, 1966). A convenient, inexpensive edition of the Convention debates is Winton U. Solberg, *The Federal Convention and the Formation of the Union of the American States* (Indianapolis: Liberal Arts Press, 1958). The older multiple-volume editions by Farrand and Elliot on the Philadelphia Constitutional Convention and the state ratifying conventions also provide heavy-handed access to Madison's speeches and the controversy over ratification. See Jonathan Elliot, ed., *The Debates in the Several State Conventions on the Adoption of the Federal Constitution as Recommended by the General Convention at Philadelphia, in 1787,* 2nd ed., 5 vols. (Philadelphia: Lippincott, 1896), and Max Farrand, ed., *The Records of the Federal Convention,* 3 vols. (New Haven: Yale University Press, 1911). For single-volume editions of Madison's writings, see Marvin Meyers, ed., *The Mind of the Founder: Sources of the Political Thought of James Madison,* rev. ed. (Hanover, N.H.: University Press of New England, 1981); Merrill D. Peterson, ed., *James Madison: A Biography in His Own Words* (New York:

Newsweek/Harper & Row, 1974); and Saul Padover, *The Forging of American Federalism: Selected Writings of James Madison* (New York: Harper Torchbooks, 1966). There are a number of handy editions of *The Federalist* in paperback. A careful edition is that by Jacob E. Cooke, ed., *The Federalist* (Middletown, Conn.: Wesleyan University Press, 1961), which is also a Meridian paperback. An excellent edition, and one with a superb book-length introduction, is Benjamin Wright, *The Federalist* (Cambridge, Mass.: Belknap Press of Harvard Univerity Press, 1961).

Index

Accommodation, concept of, 160-162

Adair, Douglass, 18, 32, 33, 168, 169, 177, 184, 185

Adams, Henry, 183

Adams, John, 32, 140

Alien and Sedition Acts (1798-1800), 10, 42, 191; consequences of, 15; and interposition, 16; Madison against, 4-5, 7-8, 10, 16, 17, 92-93, 145-146, 152, 155; and Madison's republicanism, 66-67, 87, 89-90, 132, 140-141; and majority faction, 109; in violation of constitution, 153; and Virginia Resolutions, 147-148 (*see also* Sedition Act)

Althusius, Johannes, 31, 169

American nationality, 86

American Revolution, 27, 30, 44, 132, 134, 137; political theory of, 24

Ames, Fisher, 122

Ammon, Harry, 191

Amplitude of national power, 77, 78, 80-83, 103, 111, 118-119

Anarchy, 15, 52, 55, 56, 64

Annapolis Convention, 51, 134-135

Anti-Federalists, 79, 187; and extensive republic, 33; as men of little faith, 187

Anti-republicanism, 2, 3, 46, 48, 90, 93, 94, 160, 163; and Calhoun's political theory, 55-56; Madison's analysis of, 133-142; and suffrage, 126-128

Appleby, Joyce, 191

Aristotle, 18, 19, 24, 29, 30, 44, 104, 168, 169

Articles of Confederation, 1, 2, 14, 28, 51, 57, 58, 62, 63, 74, 96, 109, 110, 187; consequences of, 15, 26, 69; and Constitution, 98; and faction, 103, 119; Madison on, 1-2, 48-51, 69-75; and nullification and secession, 54-56

Assembly, freedom of, 112, 150, 154, 161

Bailyn, Bernard, 185

Bank bill, 90, 140, 145

Barry, W. T., 172

Beard, Charles, 110, 177, 188, 189

Bennett, Walter H., 189

Benson, George, 190

Bentley, Arthur E., 189

Bill for Religious Freedom, 14-15

Bill of Rights, 4, 5, 6, 26, 138-139, 155

Blacks: in modern America, 164; and suffrage, 126-127

Bonus Bill of 1817, 93

Brant, Irving, 16-17, 167, 168, 173, 175, 183, 185, 187

Brown, Robert E., 188

Brown, Stuart Gerry, 175, 185, 187

Burns, Edward McNall, 185

Burns, James MacGregor, 190

Cabell, Joseph C., 176, 181

Calculated risk, concept of, 163-164